I ASKED THE AUTHOR

Written by Boksoon Kim

Table of Contents

Preface iv

Major Life Events vi

Chapter 1: My Childhood 1

Chapter 2: Searching for God 18

Chapter 3: Repentance and The Baptism Of The
Holy Spirit 45

Chapter 4: There Is No Secret 51

Chapter 5: Things I will get when I serve God in
this world 55

Chapter 6: Possessed By Evil Spirits 61

Chapter 7: What is a missionary? 68

Chapter 8: The Way To Win Over Opponent 72

Chapter 9: I Am Different 82

Chapter10: Fake Missionaries 86

Chapter 11: Repentance Of Ministers 90

Chapter 12: People Who Are Curious To Know More
About Others Sin 94

Chapter 13: Prayer Has Its End 98

Chapter 14: The End Of The Age..................................106

Chapter 15: Banana Bread 120

Chapter 16: Love For The Succulents............................123

Chapter 17: God is love..127

Chapter 18: Forgiveness And Unforgiveness...................141

Preface

Once I was a little known figure, but after retirement, I have been living as a forgotten person thinking that life would finish like that. Then God visited me. He led me to write this book, which I did not intend, helped me remember forgotten events of the past, helped me put in writings to describe my thoughts and feelings, and helped me find a publisher to print the book.

When I thought about God who visited me, I thought about God who visited Abraham when Abraham was 99 years old. Abraham might have thought that his life would finish while raising Ishmael. But God visited Abraham because God was not yet done with Abraham.

So I thought that God was not done yet with me. God must have something to do with me. When I knew that God still remembers me and loves me, my heart was filled with love and happiness. Joy and strength well up from the inside of my heart. I feel like I have a second period of my best days.

I was always busy and I did not have a chance to tell my children about my past life. I want to share things I couldn't say to my children through this book.

I thank missionary Daniel Kim who advised me to write a book. I thank Judy Lim and Ebun Seuong who read this book and gave me their sincere feedback. I thank Marc

Matos. His feedback gave me encouragement and hope when I needed it. My friend, Saeyun Moon pointed out in detail the general structure and every single word. I edited everything she mentioned. I thank my dentist Augustine Kim. Although he was busy, he read this book and gave me words of encouragement. I thank missionary Mark Hong who tried to find a publisher for this book. I thank Haehun Matoes who helped me with my English writing. I thank chris@amazonpublishingnetwork.com.

I pray every day for those who read this book. I pray that God may open their hearts and souls and touch them with the Holy Spirit.

December 10, 2023 Boksoon Kim

Major Life Events

Jan. 1971	Graduated from St. Columban's School of Nursing
Jan. 1972	Completed the midwifery training at Seoul National University Hospital.
Feb. 1973	Went to NYC as a nurse lay missionary
Feb. 2003	Joined Houston CMI church
May 2006	Pastor of Houston CMI church
Jan. 2012	Retired from nursing
Feb. 2015	Graduated from Seoul International University Mdiv. master's program
Jan. 2019	Retired from the pastor position of Houston CMI church
Present	mom for succulents

Chapter 1:
My Childhood

I was born in the year of the Korean War, which lasted for three and a half years. I had no memory of the actual war, but I grew up in the rubble of the war.

Beggars knocked on our door at least once daily, if not every mealtime. They said, "Give me one spoonful of food." The orphanages were full of orphans, and it was not uncommon to see people with disabilities on the streets.

Almost every family had a casualty in the war. I heard many vivid stories of hunger, missing persons, torture, death, and public mass executions in the marketplace. More than a million people died, and those who lived had to struggle to survive.

The shortage of food was severe. I saw a truck loaded with bags of flour and corn flour with an American flag and a picture of two hands shaking on every bag. These were foods coming from America; then, I knew that my family might be able to eat for a couple of weeks. The bags of powder were distributed to every family through the village offices according to the number of family members.

Many songs expressed the pain of the war, the pain of fighting soldiers, the pain of permanent separation of husband and wife, the pain of refugee life, and the pain of no education. Among those songs, one song echoed in my mind for a long time. When I was young, I sang this song while playing with a ball. It was about a girl who wanted to go to school but couldn't because her dad couldn't pay the tuition due to poverty.

Daddy, please, send me to school.

I envy the girl on her way to school.

I envy the girl in her school uniform and a backpack on her back.

If only my mom had been alive, she would have combed my hair every morning, saying to me,

"Go to school, go to school."

Don't cry, Okja, Don't cry, Okja, my daughter, I will send you to school, even if I have to work as a laborer.

Whenever I sang this song, I felt sorry for this girl, and I thought I was luckier than she was because I went to school, at least. But my own situation was very close to that of Okja. At the end of the 1950s in Korea, students had to pay tuition to study in elementary, middle, and high schools. In elementary school, the tuition was called a 'monthly payment for teachers.' So it sounds like students had to pay monthly. Those students in middle and high school had to pay twice a year, and it was called 'tuition.' Any student who couldn't pay the tuition had to drop out.

During elementary school period - I don't remember what grade I was in - my teacher called me to come forward to his desk, which was in front of the classroom. I got up from my chair and stood in front of his desk. He asked me to go home right now and bring my monthly tuition. My tuition had not been paid. I didn't know my tuition had not been paid for just one month or several months.

It took me about 30-40 minutes to walk home from school. My mom was at home and she didn't have money. I refused to go inside my home but stayed outside the gate, crying loudly. My parents must have paid the tuition somehow afterward, seeing that I could graduate from elementary school.

Tuition was one of many problems I had in elementary school. My classmates had supplementary study books, private tutors, and extra studies after school. I had to compete with kids who had better conditions of study. I didn't have supplementary study books, private tutors, or extra studies after school. Besides, I had no one I could ask when I had a question. At least I had old, used school textbooks, which my parents bought from a used bookstore. I solved math problems in empty spaces in the newspapers.

I was either in the 3rd or 4th grade of elementary school. I was thinking about how to compete with my classmates who had better conditions than mine. I thought that kids' IQ didn't play a big role. We all had an average IQ. I had to study better than my classmates who had all kinds of advantages. How can I make a little difference between my classmates and me? To make a little difference, I had to study a little more than they did.

When they study in school, I study in school, too. When they study at home, I study at home, too. But the difference comes when I study when they don't . So, I began to look for those times when they don't study while I study.

During recess, they play outside, but I stay in the classroom and study. Here, I can make a little difference. While walking back and forth between school and home, they don't study, and I study. I can make a difference from here. While eating breakfast and dinner at home, they don't study, but I study. I hold my spoon in my right hand, and I hold a book in my left hand. I can make a little difference from here, too. I sleep well at night. I don't sacrifice my sleep for study but I maximize daylight for study. I go to bed early and get up early.

Now, I figured out what to do, I must carry on with my plan. Time will tell the results.

I woke up early and studied until I left home for school. I studied with unbelievable concentration in the morning. I ate breakfast with a book in my left hand while eating with my right hand. The hours of walking to school were my study time. During recess at school, other kids played outside, and I remained alone in the classroom. Looking at the girls playing outside, I said to myself, "Good, have fun. I'm here studying." I didn't have any study aides, but I studied the textbooks as if I were chewing them.

When I was in fourth grade, once in a while, I could see textbook pages in my mind. In my mind I saw everything written on the page, I saw the whole page clearly, just like I was looking at the pages with my eyes. I could read the whole page in my mind from the beginning to the end.

While taking an examination in school, I tapped into my mind and I could see the text book. I opened the page I wanted. I could see everything in detail, vocabularies, names, numbers, and pictures on that page. So I could answer the question in the examination. Then I turned the page in my mind, and I saw the next page also.

I didn't have this phenomenon always nor could I make it happen at will. I had this phenomenon once in a while when I concentrated during examinations. This phenomenon continued until my 2nd grade of middle school.

In my 2nd year of middle school, the whole 2nd graders gathered in the auditorium. The dancing teacher said that only one student wrote the correct answer to a question. She announced my name. The question was, "Who is the founder of modern dance?" I wrote the name Isadora Duncan. At that time I opened the book in my mind and saw the name. This was the last time I could see in my mind.

I could read in my mind not only books but also I could see the blackboard teachers wrote days ago or weeks ago. I could see the whole blackboard with numbers, lines, and circles or triangles which a teacher wrote with a chalk.

Later, when I became an adult, I learned that this phenomenon is called 'photogenic memory,'

I didn't know how and why this had happened to me, and why this had disappeared, but sure, it had helped me a lot with my examinations.

I was a poor student who had nothing, but I became 1st or 2nd in rank in the whole grade when I carried on my strategy of making a little difference. My school reports were filled with A's and I felt awkward when I saw B in physical education.

I took the entrance examination for middle school, and I was ranked in second place. The good news was that the school gives scholarships to the 1st, 2nd, and 3rd highest ranking students in the entrance examination. The tuition was paid with a scholarship, but still, my parents had to come up with the entrance fee. I didn't know how my parents were able to pay the entrance fee, but they were able to pay it. The entrance fee was the last money my parents paid for my education.

The middle school granted the scholarship to three students who were in the 1st, 2nd, and 3rd rank in the whole grade. There were about 70-80 students in one class and seven classes of the same grade. It meant that there were 500-550 students in my grade and I had to be in the top three to continue to study in school with a scholarship.

As time passed, I learned that one question determined my rank, whether to be first or second. I realized the importance of one question. I shouldn't study superficially, but I had to study with clarity and depth, with critical analysis and judgment.

After one semester in middle school, I was behind in English. My classmates had an English dictionary and English practice manuals, and they studied extra classes at the English teacher's home.

I had only one book, the English textbook. At home, I had a torn English dictionary, half of my palm in size I couldn't use. When the English teacher read sentences and paragraphs, I quickly wrote the sounds in Korean under the

English words, and I read the Korean words instead of the English words. I didn't know how to pronounce vowels and consonants. I just read the Korean words, and I wished the English class would finish soon. The English teacher always carried a long wooden stick and used it to beat us. I was scared of the stick and wrote Korean words diligently.

The first semester passed like this, and I thought about it.

"I can not go on like this any more. I must solve this English problem fundamentally. Very well! I have no money to buy an English dictionary. I can not have a tutor. Let me think about it. Let me get to the bottom of it.

What is English?

If I know the answer, I will be able to get solutions.

What is English?

English is English.

I spent one semester not knowing what English was.

I thought about English speaking natives. New born babies do not know English grammar or study English. But after 2-3 years they speak English very well. Why is that so? How do they learn English?

At that time, in Korea, English education was done as follows: an English teacher first reads sentences. Then he asks several students to read. Next the teacher cuts sentences into smaller pieces and explains the grammar. Then the students take written tests. Students study English for 3 years in middle school and 3 years in high school.

After studying English for a total of 6 years, they can not speak English. Why?

How do babies of English speaking natives learn English? Should I learn English like those babies? They learn English not through grammars but through sounds.

English is a form of communication through sounds. It is like a mutual promise of sounds. Each object and each concept has its own unique sound. By making the promised unique sound, the meaning is transferred from one person to another, and the two are able to communicate. Even though one may not know correct grammar, he can communicate when he makes a correct sound. Contrarily, one knows grammar correctly but makes a wrong sound which may give a different meaning, and the opposite person can not understand.

Here, I have concluded the definition of English.

English is sound!

English is sound!

English is sound!

Then I saw the faults of the educational system of English in Korea in my time. After studying English for3 years in middle school, 3 years in high school, 4 years of English major in college, a total of 10 years, many cannot speak in English. How wrong is it? How regrettable is it? How wasteful is it?

From that time on I knew what I should do. I will study the sound of English. After 3 years of middle school and 3 years of high school, I will speak in English and communicate in English. I won't waste my next 5 and a half years in the school system. But I will continue studying English in the school system in order to maintain my grades and my scholarship. So I started two different ways of studying English; one was according to the school system, and the other was according to my own way of focusing on sound.

At that time Choong Ang daily newspaper and Korea newspaper had English cartoons daily. I cut those cartoons and made a book. The small cartoon book was always in my hand when I walked between school and home. I had several of those cartoon books.

My pronunciation study was limited. At that time there were no TVs, computers, CDs, or foreigners. My only chance to improve my pronunciation was watching movies in English. Once in a while the school sponsored an opportunity to watch foreign movies in a movie theater. At that time I concentrated on listening to the sounds and I could hear short sentences.

Once I was walking with my father. A tall white man and a little Korean girl were standing. I said to my dad. "Daddy, stay here. I want to test my English and I will speak to the white man."

I walked to the white man and asked him. "Is she your daughter?" He smiled and answered, "Oh, no!" I made the correct sounds and the correct meaning was transferred to the man. I was pleased. I am doing the right

At that time there were many supplemental study books for English study. The most popular book was Samweeilche, meaning three in one. It seemed like everyone had the book except me. I saved money and went to the bookstore. I preferred a thin, less expensive one to a thick, expensive one. I chose a thin, inexpensive one. The author was Hyunpil Ahn.

When I study a book, I summarize it in one page of a notebook. A book is like a tree. A thick book is like a tree with many branches and leaves. A thin book is like a tree with fewer branches and leaves. But each book has one root. When I summarize one book on one page, I can see its roots and branches. With one root some authors make it a big book with a huge volume. Some authors make it a small book with simple clarity. I always prefer the latter.

Some rich students have several big, expensive books for English study. In my opinion, they are suffering from too much volume. They are lost not knowing what the root is and what the branches are. Until I graduated from high school, the next five and a half years, I studied this one book repeatedly again and again. I thoroughly learned this one book and I knew every sentence, every page in it.

After studying English for five and a half years according to my analysis and conclusion, by the end of high school, my English was far ahead of my classmates who studied with tutors, and many supplemental study books. No one was even close to my level of English.

Had my parents had money, how might I have solved my English problem? I might have asked my tutor. "Teacher, what is English?" The teacher might have answered as follows; "Well, English is the language of the British people. After the discovery of America the British came to America and settled in America. So their language became the language of America. English was originally the language of the Englo Sexon who were Germanic European. When the Englo Sexon moved to and settled in England, their language became the language of England.

Now, English is the language of the world. English is the language of international politics, economy, art, sports…etc. So you need to study English diligently. English is an essential necessity for global growth."

I am glad that I had no one to answer me like this. Because my parents had no money I had no tutor, and no one to ask, I had to find out the answer alone by myself after one semester of middle school. "What is English?" I found that English is sound.

Poverty is not always bad. There are invisible benefits that come from being poor. Money can not buy these benefits. Poverty drove me to face my troubles alone, analyze my troubles alone, find solutions alone, and finally become a winner. Poverty gave me a life as strong as weed. Whatever situation I face, whether in the desert, or in a swamp, or in danger I get up from zero, from nothing. Many who face the same situation I face, may give up. But I got up. Zero has always been my starting point.

I became a high school senior. My classmates were studying very hard to go to universities in Seoul. I also wanted to go to university in Seoul. I was able to study for the last 6 years with a scholarship. How am I able to support my education in Seoul?

At that time in my hometown Mokpo there was only one college, a two year course teacher's college. After 2 years of study in college, one has to live his or her life as an elementary school teacher.

I didn't like Mokpo even though it was my hometown. The marketplace where I used to walk and roam around, small alleys, streets and houses which were familiar in my eyes, the beach where I used to swim across the mountain Yoodal, movie theaters, street foods, love of my parents, love of my brother and sisters, kids in the neighbor, school friends…….

But the more I grew up in Mokpo, the more depressing I had in my heart. What would my future be like if I continued to live in Mokpo? I would marry a bank clerk if I am lucky. I would live and die as a housewife going after what to wear and what to eat. I observed women's life in Mokpo, born in Mokpo, lived in Mokpo, and died in Mokpo. I didn't want to live my life like that.

This suffocated me. I couldn't breathe. I will leave Mokpo. I will go out to the whole world. I will study at least 5 languages and I will learn everything about the world where I live. I will stand on top of the world. I will escape from my hometown.

For that reason, I didn't want to go to the teachers' college. The direction of my life was going out of my hometown and the teachers' college was the opposite of my life direction.

Girls from rich families went to middle schools in Seoul after elementary school. Girls from less rich families went to high schools in Seoul after graduating from middle school. The remaining girls went to colleges in Seoul after high school. The poor girls who could not even buy train tickets to Seoul remained in Mokpo and I was one of them.

I hoped vaguely to go to college in Seoul, but I faced a harsh reality when I became a senior in high school. I thought about my situation.

Can I receive a scholarship from a university in Seoul through an entrance examination? - not sure.

Can I support my tuition and living costs after entering a university in Seoul? I have to work and make enough money to cover both tuition and living costs. That could be possible through selling my body and prostitution. This is not the way to go. Even if my life may be behind, I should keep my life clean.

I came to the conclusion to remain in Mokpo and find a job. Other senior high school girls were busy preparing for the entrance examination. The high school offered extended extra two hour classes after regular daily 8 hour classes. The extra after school classes were divided into two groups, either liberal arts or science. High school senior students chose which class they would take according to their future directions. But I didn't take either class because I was not going to college. I had plenty of time and I was killing time.

I asked my sister to find a job for me because graduation was coming close. She asked me to give her a copy of the school report from the high school. I got a copy of my report card and gave it to my sister. After several days she returned my report card back to me, saying; "You are a person of study and continue your study." I had nowhere to turn. I couldn't go to college and I couldn't get a job either.

In our high school, there was another person who was idling every day in school. She was a Peace Corps teacher. Often she and I spent time together. Several months ago a Peace Corps teacher came to our high school. She had blonde hair and blue eyes. What she could do in our school was to teach English conversation after regular classes.

On the first day of her English conversation class, so many girls came and filled the classroom. There was no chair available and some had to stand. The Peace Corps teacher was very pleased and started to teach from the basics.

"How do you do?"

"How are you?"

The teacher brought her face close to the students and asked excitedly. Then the students should have responded, "I am fine, thank you. And you?" But instead, they had such a look on their faces, half fear and half laughing, and turned their faces away from the teacher, to the opposite direction from the teacher. The students seemed to see the teacher as an alien. The teacher said to me in her own words, "They look at me like a monkey in a cage."

After one month all the students quit the class except two; one girl and me. But I was the teacher's favorite. The teacher and I used to meet and have time together. I understood her difficult situation and once in a while she expressed her difficulties. At least I attended 7-8 regular classes at school, but the Peace Corps teacher had absolutely nothing to do in our school. But she took care of me to the end. I was her one and only student.

One day the Peace Corps teacher showed me a piece of paper. She said that she bought it for me. At that time there were not many foreigners in Mokpo. So, all the foreigners gathered together and she went to the meeting. From the gathering, she got this information. There was a nursing school in Mokpo which opened a year ago and was run by Catholic nuns. The school offered a full scholarship to cover both tuition and dormitory just to one top student from the entrance examination.

I didn't know how she found out that I had quit college education due to no money. I had no knowledge that there was a nursing school in Mokpo. The paper she brought was an application form for the nursing school. I started to prepare the application. Since I could neither go to college nor could I get a job, I would be a jobless idler at home. Going to a nursing school was a better choice than unemployment.

When I entered the teacher's office to receive my teacher's seal for the application, I experienced death. It seemed that the school hoped that I would go to the famous Seoul National University and bring glory to the high school. But going to an unknown nursing school in Mokpo was an unbearable shame to me.

Because of poverty, I had swallowed so much shame but going to a nursing school was not a shame but death. It was too noble to say that my self-respect fell to the ground. I died. I couldn't imagine that my life would fall this low.

I came back to my senses and began to prepare for the entrance examination. I had to be at the top to receive the scholarship. I was not sure whether I could be at the top because I heard that Catholic students from all over Korea would come to this school. I had about 3 months before the entrance examination. Suddenly I entered study mode and studied all day long. I had a habit of writing everything that I studied. When I wrote with my right hand all day long, my right arm was swollen and painful. Still, I couldn't rest but continued studying.

I took the test and the result was posted. I was the top among the 25 students. So I could continue my study with a full scholarship covering both dormitory and tuition. The school gives scholarships to only one top student and I maintained the scholarship for 3 years.

After I started nursing school, I began to know about the school. The school and the dormitory were in the same building and the school building was next to the convent of Catholic nuns. Among the nuns, there was one Korean nun and one British nun, and the majority were Irish nuns. Most of the students were Catholics and once in a while all students participated in Catholic church events.

There were no textbooks in Korean. All the nursing textbooks had been imported from abroad and written in English. We studied with those books. Korean nursing professors translated those books till late at night and taught us in Korean mixed with English vocabulary. Both the professors and the students were stressed out so much, but this was an opportunity for me. By the time I graduated, I was reading the textbooks as fast as I would read books written in Korean.

In my third year and final year of nursing school, the school offered me an exceptional suggestion. The school would send me abroad where I would study nursing for 2 years, receive a bachelor's degree in nursing, return to school, and teach for 2 years. I declined this offer.

A while later the school offered me again. This time the school asked me to teach just one year after studying abroad. Also, they would consider that my teaching would not interfere with my marriage life. I declined again.

The reason for my refusal was their offer was the opposite of my life direction. My life direction was to leave my hometown and go out into the world. For any reason, I didn't want to return to my hometown. Another reason for my refusal was that I didn't want to bind my life under a contract. By then Korean nurses went to work in West Germany. I could go abroad on my own. Why should I bind my life under a contract?

The school gave me a scholarship for 3 years, fed me, taught me, and trained me. But I coldly rejected it and chose to move on to live a life I wanted to live.

Chapter 2: Searching for God

Bang! Bang! Bang!

In the middle of the night, someone loudly knocked on the door of our home. Someone shouted, "Daeho's mom! Daeho is dead!" My dad and my mom woke up from their sleep. I also woke up from my sleep but I moved to another room to sleep continuously. But before I fell asleep, I heard the sounds of weeping and wailing of my parents. I thought, 'Oh, my brother must be dead.'

My brother finished his work and came home at around 10 pm. After eating his dinner, he went to his friend's home. My brother had a dozen friends. Once in a while, after work, they gathered at one of their homes, slept that night together, and went to work the next morning. That night, my brother left home after dinner to join the fellowship at his friend's home.

After 4- 5 hours, he came home as a corpse. His friends put his body on a blanket and carried him to our home. My dad was touching the body of my brother with the hope that he might come back to life. But my brother didn't come back to life. My home rapidly changed into a house of mourning. My brother's body was laid in the corner of the living room. His body would be buried after mourning for three days. The visitors arrived and their weeping was heard.

But I did not feel any sorrow even though my brother was dead. I was thinking about death. Trees die, birds die, animals die, and people die. I knew that. But until then death was far away from me. Death was not related to me at all. I was a spectator of death. I was watching dramas that death brings to human life.

Death came to my own family. I was no longer a spectator of death. I had to face it and deal with it.

What is death?

There is death and it indeed comes to a person.

What is death?

All my brother's possessions were brought out to the front yard and burned. His clothes, suits, love letters, stamp collections, and picture collections were burning in red flames. I knew how much he loved and cared for each one of them. But when death came to him, all of them turned to ashes.

When death comes suddenly and stops everything, should people struggle hard to live? Should I study hard when death turns everything into ashes? Should people deceive and fight to make more money? When death comes, everything stops and turns to ashes, and death comes suddenly and anytime.

The reason people deceive and are deceived, push and are pushed, beat others, and are beaten is that they do not realize the coming death. Had people realized the coming of death, they would not have hurt others to gain more. People fight, deceive, and hurt others because death is not in their minds and thoughts. People are ignorant of death and I was one of them.

Death is not just being dead. Death influences one's life on how one lives his or her life. The life of those who are aware of death is different from the life of those who are not. Had my brother known that death was coming very close to him, he would have lived a different life.

I was thinking about these things and I didn't feel sorrow.

"What is death?"

Some people rebuked me for my behavior. They wanted me to change my clothes and mourn. I was wearing red pants. I didn't pay any attention to my clothes because I was thinking about death.

On the third day of death, it was the day that my brother's body would be buried in a public cemetery. I was sitting next to my brother's dead body thinking about death. I touched his body with my finger and it was as hard as rock. The stiffness of the dead body took place. The color of his skin turned to dark gray and had a rotten smell like vinegar.

I thought about my real living brother who was talking to me, smiling at me, my brother who was alive with life. This rotting body was not my brother. My brother was the person alive who was talking and smiling at me.

I thought, 'Ah! Where did my brother go, leaving his body here?'

At that moment I realized the definition of death. Death was the separation of life and body. People are alive when life and body are united. People are dead when life and body are separated. The separation of life and body came to my brother. It took me three days to find this.

His body is here. Then where did the life of my brother go?

What is after death?

Christians say that there is heaven and hell after death.

Is that true?

If that is true, did my brother go to hell?

We were atheists. We joked about Christians.

I must find out what is after death.

But who will teach me about things after death? No human can return to life after death. There is no one in the world who can teach me about things after death.

But God knows.

God can teach me about things after death.

I made up my mind to find God to find out what is after death.

After this my mind was released from deep thoughts and I was filled with sorrow. I wept and cried for the first time on the third day of his death.

When I made a decision to find God, I was a freshman in high school in Korea. (In America a sophomore in high school) Where shall I go to find God? I thought that God would be in religion. So I decided to check each religion.

First, I excluded Buddhism. There is no God in Buddhism. It is a place where humans try to reach enlightenment through meditation and human efforts.

Secondly, I excluded one church. I had two classmates from elementary school through high school who went to that church. They were very eager to convert classmates to their faith and talked a lot about their life of faith. As an outsider, I saw some troubles from them. They refused to salute the national flags. They refused blood transfusion for medical treatment. I thought that a healthy religion wouldn't have so many troubles like these. Above all my two classmates were very selfish. They didn't lose anything for others. Seeing them in school was enough for me. I didn't want to see them on Sundays.

Thirdly, I went to a church. I don't remember how I started to go to this church. I began to study their bible with a Korean church member. The church had its own bible which was different from the regular Bible. The teacher asked me to buy their bible, so I bought one even though it was expensive to me. I studied their bible once a week at the church.

It was the third month since I went to this church. That day I wore my high school uniform holding their bible in my hand and went to the church which was on the second floor. I went up the steps to the second floor and the door was open and there was no one inside. Long chairs were placed into two sections and there was a space between these two sections so that people could pass. On the left side, there were about 3-4 small rooms. I used to study with the teacher in one of the rooms.

From the entrance, I walked about 3-4 feet. Right before I turned to the left, someone said to me,

"This is a cult."

I was terrified. Right away I turned back to the entrance and ran down the stairs to the first floor and to the outside. I stood in the middle of the street. I was relieved from fear and terror. It was a hot day and the sun was shining. But I had goosebumps in both arms all over. Every single hair stood up in my arms. I was a high school sophomore and an atheist. I did not think about a cult in religion and I was gradually falling into it. There was no one inside. Who was it who warned me by saying, "This is a cult?"

The next church I went to find God was the North Presbyterian church. North Presbyterian church was the largest church in my hometown at that time. I felt safe to go there. Originally, I planned to check every religion. But I changed that. I wanted to be safe. I went to the Sunday worship service and sat in the last row. I left as soon as the worship service was over. I didn't join any other activities at the church. I didn't intend to be a member of the church. I went there to find God. I didn't get anything from the pastor's sermon. But I continued to attend the Sunday worship services in order to meet God.

The more I attended the Sunday worship services, the more rejections accumulated in my mind. I didn't like the smiles of church members. I could not understand why they were smiling.

My heart was scorching dry, burning because I did not find God. I said to myself, 'I don't like your smiles.'

Also, I saw the hypocritical double standards from the church members. At the church they pretended that they were good believers. But outside of the church in the world, they were more worldly and selfish than non-believers. I was tired of seeing these in the church.

About 8 months had passed since I began to go to the North Presbyterian church. At the end of the worship service one person gave an announcement to the congregation.

"Today is so and so's birthday. He prepared rice cakes for you. After worship service, do not just leave. Stop by the cafeteria and enjoy the rice cakes."

When I heard this announcement, I blew up all my accumulated anger and frustration. I yelled and shouted in my mind.

"What did you say to me?

Did you ask me to eat rice cakes?

Do you think that I was coming here to eat rice cakes?

Show me your God.

Show me your God whom you believe, whom you love!

Show me!"

That was the last day with the North Presbyterian church. I could not find God. My high school grade was going down. The high school gave scholarships to the top 20 students in rank. This gave me some room to relax from school study and I studied just to maintain the scholarship. But my mind was thirsty and burning searching for God so that I may live my life for life after death.

My face became very pale. My parents took me to a doctor specializing in tuberculosis. All the tests were negative. My parents bought a box of apples. No one in the family was allowed to eat the apple but me. One by one I finished the whole box of apples.

I read from somewhere that philosopher Descartes acknowledged God. I visited old bookstores and found one very old book by Descartes. I bought it and read it. His writing about God was unclear and boring. I wasted my money.

In my life, I overcame any hardships and obstacles with determination and the power of execution. Once I decided to do something, I accomplished it. But finding God was the hardest task I had ever faced. Where should I go? What should I do to find God? I had no clue. But by any means, I had to find God. God will tell me about things after death.

At the Catholic nursing school, I resumed my search for God. I did everything that the Catholic church taught me to do. I did not want to miss anything. I prayed with a rosary three times a day. I memorized all the rosary prayers. I knelt down before the statue of Mary and stayed silently for a while. This was a silent prayer besides rosary prayers. I bought a white veil and covered my head. I attended Mass but I did not participate in the Communion because I was not a Catholic church member.

I joined the catechism class. The catechism study was mainly memorization. I memorized all that was required to memorize. I attended all the catechism classes and did not miss a single class.

One winter day there was a snowstorm. The dormitory was in the middle of the hill and the Catholic church was on top of the hill. I was walking toward the top of the hill to attend the catechism class. But the snowstorm pushed my body backward and I was pushed down the hill instead of going up. I fought back hard through the strong wind and snow and finally arrived at the Catholic church on top of the hill. On arrival, I found no one. Even the teacher did not come. I was the only one who came. I studied catechism with all my heart, but I did not find God through catechism classes.

My Catholic classmates began to approach me with smiles to receive a baptism. I said, "No. I don't believe in God in my heart. How can I confess that I believe in God when in fact I don't?" Then my friend answered, "When you confess that you believe in God during baptism, God will see your faith and God will give you faith."

When I am baptized, I confess that I believe in God. But I didn't believe in God. I wanted to believe in God but I couldn't. I want to believe in God but my mind is cold and empty. How can I confess that I believe in God when I don't? If I confess that I believe in God during baptism, isn't it a lie? Are they asking me to start a believer's life with a lie? I will believe in God when I see Him with my own two eyes.

I wanted to make a clean cut conclusion with the Catholic church. I visited a Catholic priest who was Irish. So I asked him in English.

"Father, where is God?"

He answered, "God is everywhere. He is in me, He is in you, and He is here (pointing the space between him and me)"

I answered, "Maybe in you but not in me."

I could not find God in the Catholic church and I left the Catholic church after almost 3 years of nursing school.

Almost 6 years passed since I started my journey to find God. I came to the conclusion that there is no God. Christians were the people who were pretending as if there were God. I had to make an important decision. Should I go to church pretending there is God even though there is no God? Or should I continue to live as an atheist? When I compared Christians with atheists, Christians were purer, kinder, and sincere than atheists. I discussed this with my father. My father said, "If you want to be a Christian, be a Catholic. Seeing that Catholic priests and nuns don't marry and live a sacrificial life, the Catholic church seems to be a true religion." My father knew very well about the corruption of protestant pastors. Their corruption was posted in the daily newspaper for the whole world to know. But my father didn't know that the sins of Catholic priests were kept secret and not posted in the newspaper.

When I concluded that there was no God, my mind became free. I began to drink alcohol. I also attempted smoking. But I didn't want to try again when smoke choked my throat. Drinking started with one cup of beer. From one cup I moved to two cups, then to three cups, then to one bottle, from beer to sojoo, from sojoo to stronger wines. Wines were expensive and I couldn't afford them. I drank cheap Korean makguli almost every day. When I did not drink, I could not study because I could not concentrate and my hands were shaky. When I drank, my hand shaking stopped and my agitated mind became composed and I could study.

I realized that I was becoming an alcoholic. I began to think that I should stop drinking. "I am not going to drink today." I made up my mind. I was firm with my decision of no more drinking even though my hands were shaking and my mind was agitated. Then a few minutes before the closing of the dormitory door, my body would shoot out of the gate like a bullet and run to the convenience store across the street. Waving the paper money in my hand I said to the owner of the store, "Hurry! Hurry!" He quickly gave me a bowl of makuli. I drank it all while standing and rushed back to the dormitory just in time before the closure of the gate at 8 p.m.

All my efforts to quit drinking failed. Since I had accomplished all with my willpower, I thought that I could quit drinking with my will power, too. But I couldn't. My will power was as weak as a dry straw before the monstrous desire of my body. I understood the meaning of the word; 'addiction.' Will my life end like this as an alcoholic? What a tragedy to succumb to alcohol addiction before I could live my life to its full!

Close to graduation my classmate and I began to learn social dance. There were about three hours to go out from the last class to the closing of the dormitory gate. Dinner was at 5pm and the door of the dormitory closed at 8pm. After dinner, we went to the house of the dance teacher to learn and practice social dance.

That day we didn't practice any dancing, but we were drinking and eating snacks provided by the teacher. There was a man whom I had never seen before. Then these two men suddenly changed into kidnappers, the man grabbed my friend and went outside and the dance teacher grabbed me and went outside. The dance teacher took me to the street and got a taxi to a hotel at the beach. I was helpless not knowing what to do. But I was thinking about the wisdom of our Korean ancestors. These wisdoms survived over 5000 years and were handed over to us, their descendants. There was a saying in Korean;

"Even if you are dragged into a tiger's den, you will live if you keep your mind calm and alert."

I remembered this saying and repeated it in my mind. I kept my mind calm and alert.

The hotel was like a big sized second story house. The hotel clerk opened the entrance door. After the kidnapper and I entered inside, the clerk locked the door from inside. I watched carefully how he locked it. He pushed two small metal bars, one near the doorknob and the other higher close to the top. After the clerk locked the front door, he went inside the reception area. The kidnapper was talking to him over the counter. I walked to the front door and opened the two metal bars. Then I started to run. Instantly I saw the view in front of me. To my right was the ocean, to my left was the mountain and a wide road that led to the city stretched between the ocean and the mountain. In a split second, I ran toward the mountain. The Mountain was a better place to hide than the wide-open road to the city.

It was very late at night and there was no light on the mountain. I fell, ran, fell, and ran. My knees were scratched by thorn bushes and bled. I fell over small rocks but got up right away and kept on running deep into the mountain. Then I stopped and listened. It was quiet. There were no steps of the kidnapper. When I was convinced that I was safe, I fell asleep on the spot.

When I woke up, I was lying on my own vomitus. I smelled alcohol and a nasty odor from the vomitus. The right side of my face was covered with vomitus. I was still lying and looking around. The sky was dark and blue. Numerous small stars were shining like little diamonds. Here and there snow covered all over the mountain. The ocean waves from the beach were constantly splashing back and forth. The wind was blowing from the beach all the way to the mountain, and the trees were shaking gently by the breeze. The nature was so beautiful but the humans living in it were wicked and ugly.

The chilly winter wind was blowing but I did not feel cold at all. Rather I felt warm and cozy. I was about to die from hypothermia. I lost my sense of feeling cold and felt warm and cozy. Later I learned that that's how people feel before they die from hypothermia.

There I saw who I was, and what kind of human being I was. I was the ugliest of all the ugliest. Up to that moment, I appreciated myself very highly in every aspect. But I saw who I was undeniably. I had to do something to myself. I made a vow to God whom I did not believe. "God, I will never drink again." Ever since I have never drunk for more than 50 years. I hate even the smell of alcohol. God accepted my vow and helped me keep my vow. Also, I removed alcohol and dancing permanently from my life because these two almost ruined my life. The Social drink was a toxic drink, and social dance was toxic to me.

Through this dangerous experience, I learned one lesson about men. Here is an example. In Russia a man found an orphaned baby bear. He brought the baby bear to his home and raised it like his own child. The baby bear followed him and the two became inseparable . One day the grown bear killed the man. The wild animal instinct in the bear sprang up and killed the man. The wild animal instinct was dormant in the bear and not totally disappeared from the bear.

I see the same from men. Men grow well with love, education, morality, ethics, and laws. But the wild instinct has not disappeared from men. It is dormant within men. When they snap, the wild instinct springs out, and they turn into wild beasts. When they see a closed dark space, an isolated place, a closed room ,even bathrooms, the dormant instinct comes out.

Women and girls should be watchful for every man; father, older brother, younger brother, uncle, cousins, male classmates, teachers, sport coaches, pastors, Sunday school teachers, youth ministers, Catholic priests, bosses at work, coworkers at work, men in the neighbor, police men, handyman, doctors......When this problem is under control, crimes in this world will drop significantly.

To make a long story short I was restored to school after this incident and graduated from nursing school. After graduation, I became an unemployed jobless person. I could not find a job as a nurse. My classmates whose grades were behind me were all employed. They were Catholic and were hired at Catholic hospitals.

Until that time, I lived in the school system. I lived a total of 15 years in the school system. I knew how the school system worked. In the school system, a student with the highest grade was the best. Scholarship, honor, and respect followed automatically.

For the first time, I exited the school system and moved to a society. Society was not interested in how hard I studied. Society did not care how many A's I made. No place even wanted to see my school report.

Society has its own system. It is a system of connection. People who try to be connected offer bribes and flirting. I saw this even inside of a church. In order to survive in society do I have to offer bribes and flirting? I had no money to offer bribes and I was too stiff to flirt. Once I came out of school, I had no connection to hold on.

I felt that I was betrayed. I was born in poverty and I studied very hard as a matter of life and death to change my life. But all those efforts proved to be useless. Then, I was standing alone as a jobless, unemployed person in a society where everything moved through connections.

I followed my friend and entered a midwifery training course at Seoul National University Hospital. It was a one-year course without pay. Dormitory and food were provided. At least I secured a place to sleep and food to eat for one year. At least I could leave my hometown. That was a little comfort. My classmates who were working at Catholic hospitals had their paychecks and spent their money. But I couldn't afford to buy bus tickets to go around the city. The food at the dormitory was the same the whole year; rice, radish kimchi, and bean sprouts, three meals a day, 365 days a year. The whole year that's what I ate.

During the trainee period, my life went down to the lowest bottom. At that time in Korea, we had 6 workdays a week both in school and at work. In school, we had full classes from Monday to Friday and half a day on Saturday which was 4 classes. Work in the hospital was the same, with 5 full schedules and half day schedule for Saturday. I had only one day off a week.

When I had a day off every week, I spent all day in my bunker bed in the dormitory room. I did not go out because I did not have money to buy bus fares. I was just lying on the bed, 2-3 hours on my right side, next 2-3 hours on my left, 2-3 hours on my back. I felt that my life was rotting.

Did I study so hard to arrive at this situation? What is this? Eat, sleep, work - eat, sleep, work - eat, sleep, work - eat, sleep, work - eat, sleep, work - eat, sleep, work,................

Can I call this life?

Life is empty and meaningless. Can this be life?

Living like this is like stagnated water rotting slowly. My life is rotting slowly.

Isn't 'life' to struggle, fight, and accomplish something with all my strength, with all my passion as a matter of life and death? I wanted to live my life like that. Where and how can I find such a life?

I heard that there were about 200 nurses at the dormitory of the hospital. The nurses encountered each other frequently and we knew faces even though we didn't have close friendships. One of them whose face I knew but had no friendship came to me and talked to me;

"Would you like to study the Bible?"

I answered 'yes'. Since I was done with religion, I really didn't have a desire to study the Bible but I just answered 'yes' instead of 'no.' Ever since whenever she saw me, she asked me when I would study the Bible, and I began to avoid her. I avoided her for about 3 months.

One day I saw her entering the dormitory door. I was in the middle of the long hallway and I quickly entered the bathroom to avoid her. Inside the bathroom, there were a dozen individual toilets. I entered into one of it standing and waiting for her to pass the hallway. When I thought that enough time had passed, I came out of the bathroom to the hallway. To my surprise, she was standing right there. With a big smile she welcomed me. I greeted her superficially and came to my room.

I thought about the situation. How have I arrived at this awful situation? The nurse is a stalker and I am miserable. I want to live freely and peacefully. All the trouble started when I answered 'yes' to the Bible study. There is a fault on my side, too. If I said 'yes', I should keep my word. If I don't keep my word, my word will be a lie. I should not tell a lie.

Then an amazing idea popped up in my head. Let's study the Bible just once, then I will keep my word. After that, I would say no more to the Bible study, and get rid of the stalker for good.

After this decision, I studied the Bible in the nurse's room. I didn't have a Bible, so I used her Bible and returned it. We read Gospel Mark chapter one and followed the questions from the study material. I fulfilled my one-time Bible study and kept my word. I left her room without giving my cancellation notice. I could tell it anytime.

After several days I returned to the dormitory from work. I was walking in the long hallway. Suddenly I had a desire to read the Bible. It was not a trivial desire that was passing through my mind. It was a strong, eager desire. Then began an ongoing conversation of two opinions within my heart.

"I want to read the Bible. But I don't have the Bible."

"Then borrow the Bible."

"Don't borrow it."

(Borrowing was against my rule. My rule was Don't do it if you don't have one. Don't borrow.)

"It's okay to borrow the Bible."

"It is okay to borrow." was more persuasive than "Don't borrow it." I broke my own rule of not to borrow, walked to the room of my nurse Bible teacher, and knocked on the door. She was sleeping after her night shift work. She opened the door rubbing her eyes.

"May I borrow one of your Bibles?"

She quickly turned to the inside and brought three Bibles in her hands, small, medium, and large. I picked one in the middle and came to my room. I put the Bible on my desk to read. But I didn't know where to start. Should I read from the beginning ? Or from the last page? I was in and out of churches, but I didn't read the Bible.

I remembered the Gospel Mark chapter one which I read days ago. So I began to read the Gospel Mark chapter one. As I was reading along with the verses, I couldn't read any further. I was stuck in chapter one verses 21-27.

It said that a man was possessed by an evil spirit. What? An evil spirit inside of a man? This was serious, very serious. I read a lecture written by the church leader. He wrote this part very vaguely. He should have said, 'I don't know.' if he did not know. If he knew it, he should explain it with clarity and accuracy. He wrote in neither way vaguely. I thought he didn't know about an evil spirit inside of a man.

So, I tried to figure out as much as I could. If the Bible is fiction, there is no evil spirit in a man. It may be a fake story to make the book interesting. But if the Bible is nonfiction, if the Bible is a book of truth, then there is indeed an evil spirit in a man. My father told me that there was no ghost or spirit. Things that I see with my own eyes are the things that exist. According to my father's teaching an evil spirit or ghost doesn't exist. I thought about the nurse Bible teacher. She didn't look like she knew about it.

I read Mark 1:21-27 again and again repeatedly and I almost memorized all of the words. Still, I couldn't know whether an evil spirit is in a man or not, and what it is. But I didn't give up. I must find out about it.

There was one possible way to know it and I decided to try it. It was to ask the author directly. Every author knows what he wrote about. I put my two hands over the Bible, over Mark 1:21-27, closed my eyes, and asked the author of the Bible earnestly.

"Dear God, If God who wrote this Bible exists, please, answer me. It says that there is an evil spirit in a man. What is it?"

It was an atheist's prayer to the author of the Bible. It was a very short prayer but I prayed with all my strength. After this prayer, I was exhausted and lay down on my bunker bed on my stomach with my face buried on a pillow. I felt my bed a little bit tilting and I saw the whole room while my eyes were closed and buried in the pillow.

From the four corners of the ceiling, the evil spirits were coming through the concrete walls. (They passed through metals, concrete, and wood freely.) They were spirits. One group was coming from one corner, lined up in one line, overlapping each other. Another group from another corner in the same manner. All four groups were coming from the four corners of the ceiling. All of them had a clear direction toward me, toward my back.

I was so scared and was going to shout 'mom', but I realized that my mom could not help me since she was far away in my hometown and I was in Seoul. By the time the four groups of evil spirits reached very close to my back.

Out of desperation and terror I called Jesus whom I did not believe. I called "Lord, Jesus, Lord, Jesus, Lord, Jesus."

When the evil spirits heard the name of Jesus, they were terrified and scared. They fled to the corners where they came and disappeared through the cement walls. When the evil spirits were coming toward me, they were noisy and took their time to reach my back. But when they fled, they were very fast as if an ice skater ran from one corner to the other at full speed.

When all the evil spirits fled by the name of Jesus, deep peace filled my heart. The peace was like stillness, quietness at the bottom of the deep sea where waves of the surface of the sea are not able to disturb.

While I submerged myself in this peace, the evil spirits came back again for the second time from the four corners. When I saw the evil spirits again, my mind was troubled with fears again. But I called Jesus' name. "Jesus, Lord, Jesus, Lord, Jesus, Lord." The evil spirits were terrified by the name of Jesus and fled to the corners like ice skaters. When I called Jesus first rime, I did not believe in Jesus. Out of desperation, I called. But when I called Jesus a second time, I fully believed in Jesus and I called with faith in Jesus' name because I saw how the evil spirits were scared of Jesus' name.

Then I got up from my bed and sat on my bed. I just saw the spiritual world. In this world there is a visible physical world, and there is an invisible spiritual world. All my understanding, knowledge, and views collapsed. There is an invisible spiritual world but the world does not know it.

The dormitory was located near Chongro 5 street. I heard the traffic sounds of passing cars and buses endlessly coming from Chongro 5 street. That was a visible physical world. The white cement walls of the dormitory room, desk, chairs, and bed were also a visible physical world.

And there is another world, the invisible spiritual world. There are evil spirits who are scared of the name of Jesus. The name of Jesus has authority. (Mark 1:27) I saw the evil spirits but I have no words to describe it. Something that is evil, alive, moving fast, but invisible. There are no proper words to describe it with the language of the physical world. Physical world doesn't have a concept of an invisible world.

The closest expression to describe the evil spirits is that they were like smoke, a living smoke.

The evil spirits were transparent, yet alive, animal like head yet no body. They moved fast in groups and overlapped each other.

When Jesus explained about the Holy Spirit to Nicodemus in Gospel John 3:8, Jesus used the word 'wind' because wind was the closest physical word. The Wind is invisible but exists with power and direction.

I realized that the Bible is a book written about the invisible spiritual world using human language. Human language has a limit in concept so Jesus often used parables.

I want to make one point here. Invisible spiritual world is quite different from the visible physical world. The spiritual world has no time, no limit of time, eternal world.

An angel 4000 years ago is the same after 4000 years. What God said to Abraham 4000 years ago in spirit applies to us today. Contrarily the visible physical world, the human world has time, and things change according to time. The word a king said to his subjects 4000 years ago does not apply to us today, because things changed a lot. The invisible spiritual world is an eternal world without time, while the visible physical world is changing according to time.

> So all the words written in the Bible are eternal truth. The words are spirit. (John 6:63)

> "All men are like grass,

> And all their glory is like the flowers of the field;

> The grass withers and the flowers fall, But the word of the Lord stands forever." (1Peter 1:24,25)

> These words show how the two worlds are different.

After I saw the vision of the evil spirits, I got up from my bunker bed and began to write everything that I saw. After a few days, I read it to the nurse Bible teacher. She said that I had a hallucination. Hallucination is a term used for mentally sick patients when psychiatric patients see things that do not exist. In another word, she was saying that I had a symptom of mental illness. I was speechless and dumbfounded. When I read the Bible, I was commendable. When I see the same words in spiritual eyes, it is considered a mental illness. When I found the fault of the English educational system in Korea, I was surprised to see how millions of students were following the wrong system. I was even more surprised to see my Bible teacher's response to the vision God gave me. I saw a greater fault in the word of my Bible teacher than that of the English educational system in Korea.

After a few days, I visited the church leader and read what I wrote down about my vision. He said, "The Bible says that there are the Holy Spirit and the evil spirit." He was the one who wrote vaguely about the evil spirit in his lecture. When I saw the responses of these two people, I did not talk about the vision to anyone for the next 20 years. But this was how I met God.

Some churches insist "only the words of God." Such churches forbid visions, dreams, and voices of God. These are very personal and there is a danger of falling into the wrong spiritual realm. Also, visions, dreams, and voices given by the devil can infiltrate a church and destroy that church. That's why I kept my vision of Mark 1:21-27 just for myself.

I want to clarify about visions, dreams, and voices of God. God gave us the Bible for our salvation so that whoever believes the word and obeys may be saved. One can be saved without visions, dreams, and voices of God. So for our salvation, the first is the word of the Bible, the second is the word of the Bible and the third is the word of the Bible. When the word of God is taught, preached, and proclaimed, the Holy Spirit helps to empower the word of God. When the Holy Spirit works, there are miracles, visions, dreams, and voices of God as supporters of the word of God. We have to keep this order, the word of the Bible first, and visions, and dreams as supporters for the word of God.

Personally, I received amazing spiritual blessings through the vision of Mark 1:21-27 which God gave me. Had I learned the same passage from the nurse Bible teacher, what might I have learned? How can I compare God's teaching through a vision with a teaching out of the human head? There are differences between heaven and earth. When I learn the word of God from a Bible teacher, I feel like I returned from school. When I learn the word of God from God, I feel like I returned from heaven.

I was searching for God for six years but couldn't find Him. I concluded that there is no God. Then I became corrupted. But in 7th year God came to look for me. I avoided the Bible study and hid in a bathroom. God was relentless. He made me borrow the Bible, sit before the desk, open the Bible and read Mark 1:21-27. Through the word of Mark 1:21-27 God revealed Himself as the author of the Bible.

My joy and happiness in my heart exploded like a volcano when I finally met God. During my middle school period, the whole middle school students gathered at the school ground. Maybe over a thousand students were there. The principal called my name using a microphone. I ran to the principal in front of the whole school to receive an award. I was very happy but this happiness didn't last long. After 2-3 weeks it faded and was gone.

The happiness of meeting God was quite different. It was like a volcano of happiness exploded in my heart. Everything was blown off and flew away. There was an earthquake in my heart. I was happy even though I did not have money. I was happy even though I ate rice, radish kimchi, and bean sprouts every day for the whole year. I was happy even though I was wearing old shoes. I was happy even though I was trapped in my room on my day off. The love of God filled my heart and I knew how much God loved me.

People want to be happy. People pursue happiness through money and lovers. Happiness from money and lovers is short. Money and lovers make people's bodies and minds happy temporarily but do not make people's souls happy. People gather together and have a crazy mad party but their souls become sicker and sicker. Men's souls can be happy only by God.

Men's sick souls will be healed with the blood of Jesus and be happy only with the love of Jesus. When one's soul is happy, his body and mind are happy, too. Humans have been made like that.

My past life which I felt dark, shameful, and resentful turned into glorious light under the divine Province of God. It was God's guidance that I ended up as a midwifery trainee at Seoul National University Hospital where I met the nurse Bible teacher. It was God's absolute plan that I went to the nursing school even though I considered it a tomb.

From birth till then my life changed from 'unlucky' to God's Providence. I looked at my life from birth. There was no 'by chance', or 'bad luck'. I had been living according to God's plan and leading. I faced life threatening dangerous moments several times that I could have died. When I looked at those moments again from the perspective of God's Providence, I shouldn't die before God accomplishes His plan for me. I must not die and I can not die even if I want to die. I am not allowed to die before God accomplishes His plan through my life. My life has an absolute meaning in the Providence of God. Fate changed to Providence when I met God.

Chapter 3:
Repentance and The Baptism Of The Holy Spirit

I intended to end the Bible study after just one time but the Bible study continued. After the Bible study, my Bible teacher asked me to write a journal about what I learned from the Bible study that day. So I wrote what I learned about the life of John the Baptist and his ministry. The next time we got together, I read what I wrote down. When I finished reading it, she said to me, "You are proud of yourself. Write it again and repent your sins."

I was very angry but I tried to control my anger. I screamed in my mind, "So, how good are you? Why don't you repent yourself? Go ahead, repent your own sins." Then I left her room and returned to my room.

After my anger subsided, I thought about it. Her words were not wrong. Just the words 'Repent your sins.' provoke anger to listeners. The word 'repent' shouldn't be used if people want to have a good relationship with others.

But in the Bible John the Baptist shouted, 'Repent' to the people in Judea and Jerusalem and they repented confessing their sins. I thought; 'OK. You ask me to repent, I will repent. It is not a big deal.' So I decided to repent.

I had to know what repentance is.

What is repentance?

How do I repent?

In the lecture, it was written that repentance is to change one's life direction. In another word, a person who used to live for himself starts to live for God. I did not agree with that. The Bible clearly says repentance as 'confessing their sins'. (Mark 1:5) Why is it hard to understand these words; 'confessing their sins'.?

Repentance by confessing their sins means;

I raped someone and killed the person.

I stole a neighbor's sheep.

I beat up a person and the person became disabled.

I made a widow' house and land as mine.

Repentance by changing life direction;

I was selfish and lived just for myself. From now on I will live as a Bible teacher.

I was lazy, From now on I live for God.

Is changing life direction the same as confessing their sins? No. They are not the same. When one confesses his sins, I can tell what sin he committed. When one changes his life direction, I cannot tell what sin he committed. If one lives as a Bible teacher from then on, what happens to the sins he had committed in the past? Will the sins disappear because he lives a new life?

Changing life direction was not the repentance of what the Bible teaches. It was a man-made repentance. Changing life direction is the result of repentance, and not the repentance itself. When a sinner repents by confessing his sins, he starts to live a new life as the natural consequence of repentance. At the church, all changed their life directions as their repentance,

I did not see a single person who confessed his sins. They made new decisions. The Decision is not repentance.

I did not follow the noble, popular repentance. I decided to follow the word of God, and repentance by confessing my sins.

I began to think about my sins. For three days I could not find any sins. I envied people who committed sins because they could repent easily. I started to find my sins but after three days I only found that I was sinless. I had no sin to confess. How can I repent?

I set up a system of sins and checked them one by one in detail. First, sin of adultery - Did I have sin of adultery or not? I did not go close to men and did not touch any man's hand. Second, sin of stealing - When I was young about 4-5 years old, I was passing a market place, I saw a beautiful glass and picked it in my hand. But the store owner saw it and took the cup out of my hand. Should I see it as a sin of stealing? The cup returned to the owner and I had nothing with me. So I did not count it as a sin of stealing. Third, sin of lying - From very young I tried to keep my words. People easily say a promise, easily forget it, and easily say 'I am sorry.' I thought that was not right. I knew how hard it was not to say, 'I am sorry.' Keeping my word requires extra effort, suffering, and sacrifice.

Even after this, I could not find my sins. I was very tired and exhausted. I was sitting absent-mindedly on a chair in front of my desk. Then my eyes set on the papers on the bookshelf. The papers were parts of a patients' chart used in the hospital. Except for a hospital logo it was almost blank. I used it to write letters, and I brought more recently to use for Bible study.

Not only I but also other nurses were using these papers for personal use. Nurses working in the infant room brought cans of powdered milk and ate it for themselves. Intern doctors took surgical instruments from the hospital to practice suturing. Everybody did this and I did that, too.

A question came into my mind.

"Whose papers are these?"

I answered in my mind.

"Hospital's"

Another question came.

"Why is the hospital property here?"

I answered.

"Because I brought it."

At that moment I realized that I had stolen the papers. I was shocked because I remembered the word of God, "If your right hand commits sins, cut it off." Instantly I grabbed my right wrist with my left hand. My right hand was still there. I was utterly shaken because I was a thief. I threw some used papers into a trash can and I went to the hospital right away with newer papers and placed them in their original place. I returned to my room and knelt down on my knees before God. "Lord, I am a thief. I stole hospital property."

After several days I finished my work at the hospital and returned to my dormitory room. I removed the nurse cap from my head and I was still standing in the middle of my room. I felt the wind blowing over my head. There was no fan running and the windows were all closed. Then suddenly the wind entered the top of my head, passed my head, passed my heart, and disappeared. It all happened in less than one second very quickly.

When the wind passed my heart, I felt hot and extremely holy. When the wind passed my heart, it burned all my sins in my heart. For three days I couldn't find any sin. But my heart was dirty, like the inside of sewage, like the inside of the drainpipe of a bathroom. As the wind passed, the wind burned them all. I felt holy.

I remembered the words of John the Baptist in Mark 1:8;

"I baptize you with water, but he will baptize you with the Holy Spirit."

I just experienced these words. My heart was filled with holiness and tears ran endlessly over my face. God accepted my repentance and baptized me with the Holy Spirit. I knelt down on my knees and prayed to the Lord. "Lord, I will give my life to serve you." The direction of my life was changed.

I met one person who was baptized with the Holy Spirit just like me. He was a college student in Houston and I taught him the Bible at the campus of the University of Houston. Afterward he Transferred to his hometown in Waller county. I drove about one and a half hours to the college in Waller county and continued the Bible study with him.

At that time during Bible study, he told me. He turned off the light in his room. In darkness, he confessed all the sins he had ever committed one by one to Jesus. Then wind entered through the top of his head, passed his head and heart. I understood everything he said. The Lord accepted his repentance and baptized him with the Holy Spirit.

The word 'Repent' is disappearing from church. This uncomfortable word is a link to connect God and me. Repentance restores my relationship with God. Repentance is a word of miracle to change my life from a curse to a blessing. In searching for God I visited this church and that church. No one said to me that I must repent to meet God. But I met a person who dared to tell me 'Repent your sins.' I struggled for 3 days to repent and this repentance became a turning point in my life from a rotting life to a dynamic life with God.

Chapter 4:
There Is No Secret

"There is nothing concealed that will not be disclosed, or hidden that will not be made known."

Luke 12:2

One of the reasons that people commit sin is that they believe in secret and they do not know God's judgment after death. There is no secret. Every hidden thing will be revealed. I learned this through experience.

When I worked as a midwifery trainee at Seoul National University Hospital, there was lunch in the Obstetrics and Gynecology department. The expense was paid by patients' donations given as their gratitude. The restaurant was near the hospital and it was serving exclusively for the hospital events. Doctors and nurses in the Obstetrics and Gynecology department were invited to the lunch. The interns and residents were geniuses who mostly graduated from the Seoul National University Medical School. Two residents were staring at me often. And I wanted to show them my best look.

I returned from my night shift duty. I didn't go to bed but I concentrated on preparing my look.

What clothes shall I wear? What hairstyle shall I do? At that time I had long hair covering my shoulders. I wanted to add waves to my straight long hair. So I rolled the tip of my long hair with pink hair grippers all around my hair. I kept the grippers on until right before lunch time hoping it would make nice waves.

Right before lunch time I removed the grippers one by one. I did not have a big mirror in my room so I went to the bathroom where there were large wall mirrors. It was unlike what I expected. There were gripper marks all over my hair. Then I had to remove the gripper marks from my hair. I didn't have much time left for lunch. I wet my hand with water and applied water all over my hair to make it straight. I was not sure whether the gripper marks were all gone or not. But I headed for lunch with wet hair.

On arrival at the restaurant, I saw no one. The restaurant was empty. I didn't know that it had been canceled. I walked back to the dormitory. I did not know why but I went to the room of my nurse Bible teacher and knocked on the door.

She was sleeping and woke up to my knocking sounds. She was in her pajamas when she opened the door and was very surprised to see me. She asked me seriously with an apprehensive look on her face "Are you okay?" I asked her back, "What do you mean by that?" She told me about the dream she just had. In her dream, I was dishevelling my hair. She begged me in her dream, "Please, stop touching your hair. I will give you money to go to a beauty salon to take care of your hair." But I wouldn't listen to her begging. I kept on dishevelling my hair. My look and behavior might have scared her in her dream. I did not say anything to her. I returned to my room.

How can this be?

What I did alone in my room appeared in her dream.

A thin chill spread in my mind. There is no secret.

God sees all and everything. God sees what is done in pitch darkness. God sees what is done behind closed doors. The Bible says that all hidden things will be revealed. I knelt down on my knees before God. I did not say anything. I was just awestruck because what I did alone was shown in her dream at the same time.

Because of poverty, I had a habit of hiding shameful experiences secretly. There is no secret. There is no need to hide. Let's be honest. Ever since I was learning gradually to be honest even if it is shameful.

I see people who do shameful things behind a locked door. They think that no one knew about it because no one saw what they were doing. They plot a perfect crime. They get rid of witnesses. They don't leave behind any evidence. They are careful not to be seen in surveillance cameras.

But God sees all and everything and records all without missing anything. Why does God record all? God uses it as bases of His judgment later when He judges people who had ever lived on earth. (Revelation 20:2) When a judge determines a sentence in court, he does not judge according to his feelings and rumors. He judges according to written evidence which was investigated and proved. God has a book which recorded everything that each person did openly and secretly.

Living before the eyes of God and correcting my thoughts and actions are a preparation for the future eternal world that comes after death.

But alas! Are those who have done shameful things in secret and died.

Chapter 5:
Things I will get when I serve God in this world

Meeting God and the following spiritual experiences led me to an amazing level of devotion to serve God. In order to attend all the church meetings and events I fixed my work schedule with a permanent night shift from the previous rotating schedule of day, evening, and night shifts. Rumors spread that I became crazy among friends in Seoul and in my hometown.

I began to write daily bread every day. That day I finished my night shift duty and came to my room. Usually, I ate rice, radish kimchi, and bean sprouts, washed, and went to bed. That morning I decided to write daily bread first and then go to bed. One word at the end of the daily bread was "Preach the words."

This is the word of God.

God says to me, "Preach the words."

Then I will preach the words.

How about I sleep first, and preach the words when I wake up?

But can I sleep peacefully?

I felt I couldn't sleep comfortably. So I decided to preach the word first, and then go to sleep.

Barely 2-3 months have passed since I became a Christian. What should I preach? I didn't know much since I was a baby Christian. I decided to preach what I know. I will preach Gospel Mark chapter one. I had my Bible in my hand and left my room. I began to knock on the door of each room one by one at the nurses' dormitory.

It was about 9 o'clock in the morning. It was not a suitable time to find a nurse for Bible study. Day shift nurses were out at the hospital. Night shift nurses just went to bed. Evening shift nurses might be still sleeping or up eating and washing.

If I had had any tiny desire not to obey God's word, I would have excused myself like this; 'Lord, I want to preach the words, but the present hour is not suitable. I will obey you next time.'

But I had a desire to do what the Lord says. I continued knocking on each and every door. I finished all the rooms on the second floor and I went down to the first floor. Surprisingly I got a response from one room.

"Come in!"

I opened the door and entered the room. Two nurses were sitting on one bed. I knew both of them though I didn't have a friendship with them. One of them came from a family who had Christian pastors for generations. She was attending the most prestigious seminary in Korea during the day and working at night. She asked me;

"Miss Yun, why have you come?"

I answered, "I have come to teach the Bible."

She asked me, "Miss Yun, do you know the meaning of this word xxxxxxxx?"

I had never heard that Korean word before. But I thought that the word came from theology. I answered, "No." She said, "You even don't know the word, and you want to teach the Bible?"

I said. "I am sorry." I turned around, closed the door, and left the room.

I felt as if my head was hit not by a hammer, but by a huge rock. I never had such an insult in my life. She could just say, 'No.' Should she swing an iron hammer to knock me down?

I returned to my room with a stupefied mind. I sat down on a chair before my desk. I began to hit my desk with two fists in anger, shouting, crying, and screaming. Pounding with two fists was not enough. I added my right leg and banged the floor with my right leg. I was screaming, crying, and banging with both fists and my right leg.

Then I raised my right arm toward the ceiling. With my index finger pointing toward the ceiling I protested to God.

"Lord, it is all your fault. Up until this morning, my life was decent. I didn't bother others and others didn't bother me. But this morning You said to me, "Preach the words." I obeyed You without sleeping. See what happened to me when I obeyed You? I was rejected, insulted, and humiliated. It is all Your fault."

I suddenly stopped everything and became very quiet. The Lord was speaking to me. The Lord broke His silence to answer my adamant protest.

"When you serve me, you will get these things. Do you still want to serve me?"

The voice of the Lord was very casual like a voice of a father, like a father speaks to his daughter. I was quiet and couldn't say anything. Tears and anger were all gone. I repeated what the Lord said to me in my heart.

'When you serve me, you will get these things. Do you still want to serve me?"

The Lord saw, heard, and knew everything that had happened that morning. When I serve the Lord, I will get rejection, insult, shame, and humiliation. Then who wants to serve the Lord?

When I left my room holding the Bible in my hand, I was proud of myself. I roughly counted the number of people who might have read that day's daily bread. It was about 3000. What was on their minds when they read the words, "Preach the words." Oh, this is Timothy, what chapter, what verse. Then they close the Bible and the daily bread booklet. They just add another Bible knowledge to their head. Then they think they know the word.

But how many people took the Bible in their hand and went out to preach the words to obey God from their hearts? That's why I was proud of myself and I expected acknowledgement and respect. That was my own thought and my own imagination.

But in reality, I got these things - rejection, insults, humiliation - when I preached the word. Then who is willing to serve God? Shouldn't people receive recognition, glory, and riches when they serve God? God mentioned none of the good stuff but promised only suffering. I answered to the Lord, "Lord, I will serve You even though I get these things when I serve You."

Back at home, I did not serve my parents with the expectation of a good return. I served my parents because I loved them. I will serve the Lord because I love my Lord.

Since then I felt like I had an iron face. I did not have furious anger when people rejected, insulted, and humiliated me when I asked them to have Bible study with me. Those were expected responses and above all God promised me those things. I just brushed them off and moved to the next person.

After this, I thought about who God is. I thought that God was very honest. In the world, it is the opposite. People promise only good things when they recruit others. If you join us, you will make this much money, promotion, and so many benefits. But they don't reveal the bad side of the group. Lured by good promises people join the group or get married. After time passes, bad things are revealed one by one. Some are able to exit, but after 10 or 20 years people are trapped and stuck. This is the world of humans.

From the beginning upfront, God promised sufferings when He recruited me to His service. When you serve me, you will get rejection, shame, insult, and humiliation. Do you still want to serve me? There was not even a minimum wage payment. Only suffering was guaranteed. God is honest. I love the Lord who is honest. However, as I serve the Lord, the good things are added year after year. The future glory will be beyond imagination. (Romans 8:18)

Chapter 6:
Possessed By Evil Spirits

I was at the leaders' meeting. The church leader asked me to come out and stand in front of all that I did. He also asked a brother who was not married to come forward. The leader mentioned something about me but he mentioned more about the brother in length. I didn't exactly know what was going on but this often happened when the church arranged a marriage between a brother and a sister. So I began to think whether I was going to marry this brother. But soon after he married another sister.

A while later one brother came to me and gave me a book. That book belonged to another brother who asked me to give the book to the owner. Then he talked about how wonderful and great the book owner was. I immediately knew that this was a setup and I might be being watched. I had to meet the owner of the book to return the book as I was asked and I did not like such a manipulation . Marriage should be a personal matter and be dealt with respect.

I thought, 'Okay. Do whatever you want to do. I decided on my own marriage. I decide my own future. I made a vow to the Lord to serve the Lord as a single and not to marry. Because this vow was real and truthful before God, I began to think how I might serve God as a single.

But as time passed, my desire to get married was growing. Before the vow, I was free from marriage. I thought I could serve the Lord either way with marriage or without marriage. But after the vow, after marriage became forbidden, a desire for marriage was growing stronger and stronger. I never thought about this surprising turn in me, a human desire to want to do more when forbidden.

When I was a nursing student, I went to a mental hospital to have clinical experience as required by the curriculum. An old maid, single, came to me and asked me, "What is amniotic fluid?" I assumed that her mental illness was related to sex and marriage. Her image came into my mind and I began to worry whether I would become like her.

I realized that I could not keep the vow I made to God. I read the Bible to find a possibility of nullifying my vow. I felt that I would go to hell if I canceled the vow and got married. The Bible became a scary book. The more I read the Bible, the greater God's wrath and punishment to those who ignored and disobeyed God. I was full of fear.

Of course, I believed in the forgiveness of Jesus, but the following passage held me guilty.

"All the sins and blasphemies of men will be forgiven them. But whoever blasphemes against the Holy Spirit will never be forgiven."

I had to figure out whether a cancellation of a vow would be counted as a sin against the Holy Spirit or not. I began to think it was a sin against the Holy Spirit and fear of going to hell increased in me.

Then I was holding the words of Romans 8:1

"Therefore, there is now no condemnation for those who are in Christ Jesus."

I read this verse numerous times in the middle of fear of going to hell. There was a war within me. Hell was pulling me from one side and salvation was pulling me from the other side.

I began to notice some weird things going on in me. I had a severe headache. I did not have any headaches up to that time. The headache was concentrated on the lower back of my head above my neck. When the pain was severe, I wished to cut that part out with a knife.

Then I noticed that something or someone was within me besides myself.

At night I was walking in the street. I stopped and I was gazing at the top of the building. The building was maybe 10-15 stories high. Someone within me smiled and gave me a message; "Go up to the top and jump down. It is very good." I was smiling, too, thinking, 'Should I go up there and jump? I smiled and something in me smiled, too.

At that time in Seoul subway construction was going on. The middle of the street was dug down deeply and buses were passing on the narrow spaces on both sides of the street. I was sitting on the window side of a bus and I could see the deeply dug bottom of the street. Something in me smiled and said, "Jump down. It's good." I felt the same way but I couldn't jump because I was inside of a bus.

Once I threw my body toward a running bus because something in me smiled and asked me to run to the fast coming bus. Right before my body almost hit the side of the coming bus, I came to my right mind. I stopped my running body with my left hand in a split second. I was startled by what I was doing.

I also became very sensitive. I knew who was making fun of me, who was criticizing me, who was indifferent to me, who was praying for me. Only one person was praying for me. I didn't have to see each person face to face. I just knew each heart from far away.

When Jesus was in a synagogue, the Pharisees and the crowd did not know who Jesus was. But the man with an evil spirit knew that Jesus was the Son of the Most High. What the evil spirit knew, the possessed man knew. What the evil spirit knew, I knew.

I diagnosed my symptoms as being possessed by evil spirits. I learned that from the words of Mark 1:21-27. With the knowledge of Mark 1:21-27 I could diagnose my condition. That's why I did not take even one tablet of Tylenol despite the severe headache. Medicine or any other therapy was not a solution, but the name of Jesus. I was not totally under the control of the evil spirits, but I still retained the right mind to think.

Then, how can I drive these evil spirits out of me?

In Mark 1:21-27 Jesus had authority over evil spirits. Jesus ordered the evil spirits, "Come out of him." and the evil spirits came out of the man. So I commanded in the name of Jesus pointing at myself with my finger, "Come out of me." but the evil spirits did not come out of me. I repeated many times to no avail.

When I was struggling with the evil spirits, the church gave me the title of 'Samsoon who gave her body to passion.' No one knew my struggle. They were making fun of me. The Church was focused on the number of Sunday worship service attendants and the number of church membership.

One day I had a dream after many scary and crazy days passed. In my dream, there was a house burning in fire. Red flames of fire were coming out through the top of the roof and windows. Because of the fire, skinny black figures like humans were coming out of the burning house in one line. They were as skinny as chopsticks and their hands were tied with a rope like prisoners one after another. They kept on coming out in one line endlessly. I did not see the end of them. My dream was full of black and red in color. Dream is out of my control but God gives me a hint.

When I woke up, I knew that the evil spirits would come out that day. I was determined to do my part. The part I had to do was to speak out about my problem. I couldn't talk about it because it was too shameful to talk about and I kept it secret. The unspeakable secret with the increasing stresses and agony provided a cozy room for the evil spirits to stay in my mind. I had to break this cozy room where the evil spirits were hiding and living, and it was my job that I had to do but no one else.

In the morning I visited the church leader and asked him, "Can I get married?"

This meant, "Can I break my vow and get married?" Saying this to him was harder than death but I had to say this to save myself. He was the one who was testing me with marriage. I became rebellious to his handling of the matter and I went down almost to hell. He didn't say anything, and I didn't say any more. I wept for a long time on the spot.

I did not say another sentence or a lengthy explanation. One short sentence was enough to break the cozy room of the evil spirits. Like water gushing out through a broken dam, all the evil spirits were drained out. They lost a hiding place in my mind. Since then, all crazy symptoms disappeared. The headache was gone. The smiles which controlled my mind and tried to kill me were gone. The evil spirits left me. The Lord saved me again this time from the evil spirits. Since then more than 50 years passed, and the evil spirits never could make a room in me again. Since then I was more open and learned to share my troubles and joys. I have friends.

Our mind is like a bowl. The bowl of our mind is always filled with something we put into it.

What we see, think, read, hear goes to the bowl of mind. Those who play violent video games put violence into their minds. Those who pursue sex put desires of flesh into their minds. Those who hate put hatred, those who are greedy, put greed.

Those who love put love, those who seek wisdom, have wise minds, and those who love truth, have pure minds.

It is 'I' who fills the bowl of my mind. It is a matter of choice, a matter of choosing good or evil. It is not a matter of intelligence but a matter of conscience.

Our minds are wide open and exposed to the invisible spiritual world. There is no wall, no lock to keep our minds safe. Evil spirits roam around and when they find a suitable dirty bowl of mind, they make their home in that bowl of mind which we call 'possessed.' When one repents his sins, by confessing his sins, the Holy Spirit comes and touches the repented mind to make it holy.

Once possessed, that person is put on medication and will be in and out of hospital for the rest of his life. That could have been my life. But thank God. I studied Mark 1:21-27 with God and I was able to free myself from the evil spirits with the name of Jesus.

When we lose the health of our physical body, we lose all. When we lose the health of mind, we lose all as well. Information for physical health is overflowing. But information for the health of the mind is little known. I am sharing my journey into this little known danger.

Chapter 7:
What is a missionary?

The Lord had said to Abram, "Leave your country, your people and your father's household and go to the land I will show you.

"I will make you into a great nation and I will bless you; I will make your name great, and you will be a blessing. I will bless those who bless you, and whoever curses you I will curse; and all peoples on earth will be blessed through you."

Genesis 12:1-3

When I studied these words I prayed that the Lord may send me to a land I should go. While praying I worried what if I went to Africa alone, and I hoped that I would go to Germany. I studied German as a second foreign language in high school and I wanted to study in Germany. But God opened a way to America. So I went to America as a nurse lay missionary when I was 24 years old.

Finally, the airplane I was on left Kimpo airport in Korea to the United States of America. For some reason, the airplane stopped at one of the airports in Japan while all the passengers stayed inside. I saw some Japanese flight attendants coming and going. They were very stylish.

After the plane left Japan, the plane began a ten hour long flight to America.

Then I could shake off all kinds of thoughts and feelings and I began to think about my future.

'Now, I am on my way to America as a missionary. What kind of future is waiting for me?'

By then I knew a little bit about how people live their lives. When I was very young, I was sitting on my dad's lap. He just turned over 50 years old and said to me; "Future 50 years seem to be a long time. But I feel the past 50 years I have lived seem to be very short, like a few weeks or a few months."

I thought about the meaning of his words for many years as I grew. It meant that the time of 50,60,70 years would pass very fast. Life time passes very quickly, and time will come when people feel empty in their lives having accomplished nothing. My father lived like that and most people live like that.

Another side of the meaning of this word is that even though time is limited, it is just enough to accomplish one thing when one concentrates on one thing day by day during a lifetime. A lifetime of 50, 60, 70 years is given to each person to accomplish one thing. Time is not given unlimitedly.

I was on my way to America as a missionary. One of either life was waiting for me. If I use my mind, money, and time to do things right and left whatever I like, to involve myself in every trivial thing, my time of 30, 40 years as a missionary will pass quickly, and I will feel empty with my life like my father. But if I set one goal and focus on it each day for the next 30,40 years as a missionary, I will accomplish something and I will be satisfied with my life.

Life is like a train. A train starts to run and when it arrives at the final destination, it ends up running and it goes to a garage to rest. Life is once. Life has one opportunity to live. I did not want to live an empty life. I wanted to live my life to accomplish one thing and finish my life with satisfaction.

So I began to think about my future life as a missionary.

'What is a missionary?'

Inside the airplane, I did not have any research material, no dictionary, and no one who spoke with stereotyped opinions. I had to find out the definition within the scope of my knowledge and experiences.

Missionary lives alone in a foreign country. He encounters many difficult situations often with no one to help him. He has to find a job to support himself and his family in a foreign country. Sometimes he becomes sick. He has to learn a new language and teach the words of God, the Bible.

The most important thing is not to be impoverished spiritually. There are abundant spiritual foods in South Korea. There are many preachers who have in-depth knowledge of the words of God and give inspiring sermons. By keeping eyes open one can receive spiritual food. By sitting down with ears open, one can receive the word of

God. Believers can grow strong in faith by such spoon feeding.

It is not the same in foreign nations outside of South Korea. America is not a place where I can receive spiritual food by opening my eyes and ears. Spoon feeding is not available. I imagined the possibility of my dry impoverished soul falling into deep darkness. It was scary. A missionary has to be independent spiritually. I have to prepare the words of God myself, enrich myself first, and then share the spiritual food with others out of my own abundance. That's a missionary.

Everything was clear and I knew what I had to do. I did not know how many years would be given to me in the future as a missionary. Regardless, I would do one thing. I would meditate on the word of God and teach others during the time given to me in the future. Future 30-40 years seems to be a long time, but once it passes it would be like a few weeks or a few months.

I put this into practice right away. That day, 2-28-1973, I was busy with my departure. I did not study the words of daily bread. I took out my Bible and the daily bread booklet. I put them on the table which was attached to the back of the front seat to study. 'I will be self-sufficient in spiritual food.' My missionary life started from inside the airplane to America.

Chapter 8: The Way To Win Over Opponent

When there are conflicts between two parties, the common method people often use is becoming like gathering bees. It is to gather more people to their side and make louder voices than their opponent. Some use a megaphone or amplifier or social media to be louder.

This method often fails to be true and ideal, yet the world has been rolling and running with this method. In the Bible, the religious leaders in Jesus' time used this method. They instigated the crowd and made them shout loudly to crucify Jesus. (Matthew 27:22,23, Mark 15:13, Luke 23:20, John 19:6) Facing the loud shouting of the crowd, the Roman governor had to compromise. This is a method of winning with more people and louder voices regardless of truthfulness.

When there is a conflict between two individuals, who wins? One day I was working at work. During work, my nursing director called me to her office. She was a young white woman and I did not know her age. I went to her office and she told me;

"Kim, I know you have a lot of life experience. I'm having an argument with this patient and I want to listen to your opinion."

I was humbled by her invitation. In most hospitals, there is white solidarity. White doctors and white nurses have a strong solidarity which is very subtle and unseen. They keep a distance from other colored people. Then a white nursing director wanted to seek my advice. The Pharaoh of Egypt asked Joseph's advice who was a foreigner slave and prisoner. I felt a similar situation on a smaller scale. After I listened to her story I answered;

"You will not win this argument with the patient. The patient has his argument based on hospital rules. You argue based on the authority of the nursing director. Hospital rule is stronger than the authority of the nursing director. If I were you, I would apologize to the patient and finish the matter as soon as possible."

Afterwards the nursing director worked continuously and the patient was quiet. I believe that it was resolved. When there is a dispute between two individuals, winning depends on the authority of the base on which a person stands. The decision of the Supreme Court overrules the decision of the district court.

The highest authority is the words of God. The words of God have God's power and God's promise. The one who stands on God's word will be the winner. No one can defeat me when I fight with the word of God.

I will share my experience. In 1975 I was in NYC. A new director for the church in NYC just arrived from Korea. A few days after his arrival he, his wife, and I were in a room. He asked me to bring him the balance book of the church offerings and I kept the balance book. I gave him the balance book and he pretended to check it by turning a few pages. Then he put the balance book on a table nearby and asked me to stretch out my two hands which I did. He grabbed a wooden stick next to him and hit my palms 2-3 times with the stick. I heard his wife's laughing sounds. It happened very quickly and unexpectedly. This was obviously planned and intended because the wooden stick I did not see before was there, and he did not point out what part of the balance book was wrong.

I did not say anything. I returned to my apartment and began to pack. Someone borrowed my suitcase to go to Korea and I did not have any suitcase to pack. I used a small flat ramen box to pack. I placed a nursing uniform, a pair of nursing shoes, some underwear, and my nursing license. And the ramen box was full. I took all the cash I had. I left the rest of my belongings there.

My apartment was at W.12th in Manhattan and I got a taxi. I said to the taxi driver, "Let's go to the Kennedy airport." I paid the fare when I arrived at the airport. It was very late at night and most airline counters were closed. I counted my cash in hand. I had $86 with me. I didn't know where to go. I did not plan to go anywhere, yet I had to go somewhere. It was reckless just to go to a new place by myself in America.

I chose to be safe. I decided to go where my nursing school classmates lived. One lived in Tulsa, Oklahoma. Two lived in Toledo, Ohio. After I met God, I cut relationships with them, but I needed their help. But I didn't know to whom I should go. The money will decide. I prayed to the Lord to lead me to a place where I could serve Him. And I fell asleep on the chair in the lobby.

The airline counters opened very early. One way flight fee to Toledo was around $80. And over $100 to Tulsa. So with the money I had decided where to go. I was able to buy a one way ticket to Toledo, Ohio.

I was thinking with what intention the new director beat me. One reason was for sure. He would make me a person who obeys him whatever he says. In church, there is a woman next to a church leader. She considers the word of the church leader's word as the word of God. To such a woman obeying the word of a church leader is good, disobeying is evil. She eventually loses a discernment of good and evil. Such a woman should know that the church leader would dismiss and ignore her after using her.

I made up my mind to take revenge on him. "You, son of a bitch! Do I look like an easy target for you? I have an upper hand than yours. From whom did you learn beating up people in the name of God? I am not a person who can be tamed by beating. I am a person who can be tamed by the words of God, you, son of a bitch!"

When I say that I am going to take revenge on him, it doesn't mean that I do something bad to hurt him. I will compete with him in good faith. I will work harder, struggle harder than he does, and grow far greater than he does. I will make him respect me, honor me, and envy me from far away. I will make him dare not to come close to me. When he tries to trail behind me from far away, I will proclaim my victory over him. This is the way I win over a person who is in dispute with me.

My two friends in Toledo welcomed me to their apartment and I could settle in Toledo, Ohio. It took me about 2-3 weeks to change my NY state nursing license to the state of Ohio. With the nursing license of Ohio, I left my friends and moved to a space of mine. It was an attic space with one bed, a small bathroom, and no kitchen. The rent was $65 a month. The rent of a one bedroom apartment was about $200 - $250 a month. I chose to stay in a cheap place to save money and restore financially.

It was tough to start with nothing. I ate only white bread, strawberry jelly, and apples for 6 months because there was no kitchen. I walked to work for one hour and after work, I walked another hour back to my attic room. I had to pass through the downtown dangerous areas after 11 pm at night. But with God's protection, no harm touched me.

Winter was a problem. Snow piled up to my knees. My pants and shoes were wet while walking over knee high snow. I carried my nursing uniform and shoes in my bag and walked for one hour on the wet snowy street. When I arrived at the hospital, I changed into a dry uniform and shoes. After work, I walked back one hour in the darkness of the winter night.

When I saved enough money to make a downpayment to buy a car, I bought a new car with a loan. With a temporary permit, I began to drive alone, which was against the law. But I was in a dire situation, I had to drive without a driver's license. After a month, I passed the driver's license test and got my driver's license.

The attic space was like a jail room: one metal bed with an uneven mattress under an angled space, a sink, toilet, and bathtub in the next space. There was no desk, no chair, no closet. It was a perfect place to have depression.

But my heart was full of hope because I was holding the words of God, Isaiah 54:1-5 in my heart.

"Sing, O barren woman, you who never bore a child; burst into song, shout for joy, you who were never in labor; because more are the children of the desolate woman than of her who has a husband." says the Lord.

Enlarge the place of your tent, stretch your tent curtains wide, do not hold back; lengthen your cords, strengthen your stakes. For you will spread out to the right and to the left; Your descendants will dispossess nations and settle in their desolate cities.

Do not be afraid; you will not suffer shame, Do not fear disgrace; you will not be humiliated. You will forget the shame of your youth and remember no more the reproach of your widowhood.

For your Maker is your husband - the Lord Almighty is his name - The Holy One of Israel is your Redeemer; He is called the God of all the earth."

These are the words God gave the Israelites who went to Babylon as captives. I was exactly in the same situation. I had nothing and lost everything except one ramen box. I was alone with a wounded heart and felt hopeless in the attic room. I was a barren woman with no fruits. God's promises to a barren woman were amazing beyond imagination, too good to believe. I decided to believe these amazing promises. These blessings will be mine. I will rise again based on these words. I will rise again from my pain and wounds. I will rise again from nothing when God keeps these promises to me in Isaiah 45:1-5. I will do exactly what God asks me to do through Isaiah 45:1-5.

A lonely, shameful woman tends to be shrunk, self-pitiful, depressed, and inactive. But she needs to divert her energy positively, actively, and outwardly. She needs to get up and move, keep on moving to set up her tent and lengthen the cords of her tent so that her tent may be wider and bigger to the right, and to the left. God is ready to bless her, but she has to make her own tent to receive the blessings. The blessing will come not as a windfall fortune but gradually, progressively through the work of her hands. The more she widens her tent, the more blessings she will receive according to her capacity.

In my case setting a tent and widening tent cords were praying, teaching the words of God, and raising spiritual children one by one. God was more than ready to bless me and to restore all I lost if I obeyed these amazing words of Isaiah 54:1-5.

But I had no one for me to teach the Bible in Toledo because I was new to this city. Then should I stay doing nothing? I thought about this situation. I found that there was no rule in the Bible that I should teach the Bible only in the city I live in. Limiting the area was in my own thoughts, thinking I should teach the Bible to someone living in the same city. There was no such limit in the Bible. I could teach the Bible to people in another city, in another state, or in another country. The limit within my city was removed. I could reach someone as long as I could by driving.

I checked outside of Toledo. I found a Korean couple living in Cleveland. They accepted Bible study with me. After 8 hours of work at the hospital, I drove to Cleveland. It took about 2.5 or 3 hours to arrive there and arrived at around 7 p.m. in the evening. They prepared dinner and waited for me. After dinner, we studied the Bible beginning with Genesis chapter one. After the Bible study, I drove back 3 hours and arrived at my attic room at around 1 am in the middle of the night. I slept a few hours and got up at 5 am to get ready to go to work.

The Korean couple began to receive the words of God and invited others to Bible study in their apartment. So there were two groups. From that time on I drove to Cleveland twice a week to teach the Bible. My tent was widening and my tent cords were lengthening. One day I finished the Bible study in Cleveland and returned to my attic room at around 1 am at night. The Human body has a limit. It seemed like my body did not know what to do when my body had to endure sufferings beyond its limit. I and my body didn't know what to do. Tiredness is limited in its meaning. In my body, every single cell was alive while my body was aching with pain. I had to sleep a little bit and get up for work. But I couldn't go to sleep because every cell in my body was active and alive with exhaustion and pain. I knelt down on my knees, drenching my face with tears. I prayed;

"Lord, I have to sleep a little bit and get up for work. But I am too tired to sleep. Help me sleep."

After the prayer, while I was still kneeling on my knees, power spread to my whole body. Instantly my whole body turned calm, soothing, and peaceful. I lay down in my bed. I felt like lying on piles of feathers, like lying on clouds. Feeling soft, peaceful, and heavenly I fell asleep soon like an infant baby.

When I drove back and forth to Cleveland, I prayed to the Lord;

"Lord, I live in Toledo but I have two groups of Bible study in Cleveland. Grant me Bible students in Toledo."

Later the Lord granted me Bible students in Toledo, and I had one group for the Bible study in Toledo.

The husband of the Korean couple in Cleveland had an engineer's job offer from a company located in NY city. Then I asked them to move to Toledo to serve the ministry together with me. The NY company offered an annual salary of $50,000. In today's money, it would be $150,000 or $ 200,000. I could not offer any money. I could only guarantee hardships and suffering. I could show them only the attic room.

I had no money and nothing to show them. But for two reasons I invited them to move to Toledo instead of moving to NY. One reason was for them. They would become an ancestor of faith in the future church in Toledo. Abraham received special love from the Lord, and he became the father of faith, an example of faith for all believers. This was a unique opportunity of blessing to be an ancestor of faith and they would receive love and blessings in the future. I wanted them to grab this opportunity.

Another reason for inviting them was for me. I would have them as my coworkers. Finding a coworker in the mission field is like finding ten thousand war horses on a battlefield. When two coworkers serve the Lord in one heart, they make a vessel to receive the Holy Spirit. It is the shortest successful way to build a church.

The Korean couple chose the engineering job in NY and left Cleveland. After their departure, I did not go to Cleveland anymore and concentrated on Bible studies in Toledo. As time passed God's promises and blessings were fulfilled in reality. Spiritual sons and daughters were growing and the church was stretching to the right and to the left.

After several years I met the wife of the couple during a church conference. She said to me; "I should have listened to you. We should have moved to Toledo instead of NY."

She saw how much God blessed the ministry in Toledo. She saw many of my spiritual sons and daughters. I just listened to her but did not ask her why she regretted their decision to go to NY. Later through a grape vine, I heard their terrible sufferings in NY. They didn't know and I didn't know that terrible sufferings were waiting for them in NY. Since then I have seen so many, many, many people who decide their future following money. People should follow God when they decide their future.

In this way, I won over the new director who beat me. I had a landslide victory over him.

I won because in the conflict I stood on the highest authority which is the word of God. Can a human motive win over the authority of the word of God?

Chapter 9:
I Am Different

That day was my day off from work. I could leave home earlier than usual to go to a Bible study in another city. After I finished the Bible study, I was driving to return home in Toledo, and I ran out of gas in my car on a highway. Luckily, I was able to reach a nearby gas station.

When I left home in the morning, I had no cash with me, so I just grabbed my checkbook and left. At that time there was no credit card in use and only cash or checks were used to buy and pay. When I saw the gas gauge needle showing gas in the tank, I just hoped that I could make the round trip for the Bible study. But I ran out of gas on the way home.

I wrote $5 in my personal check and attempted to buy gas with the check. The gas station attendant refused to accept it. No personal check was accepted to sell gas. It was their policy.

I turned around, and walked to a nearby lawn and sat there.

"What shall I do? I don't have cash. Check is not accepted, and there is no gas in my car....."

That day one gallon of gas was 36 cents. I might be able to go home with one dollar's worth of gas. Gas with two dollars should be more than enough to go home. I prayed sitting on the lawn; "Lord, help me go home."

After the prayer, holding the $5 check in my hand, I walked toward the gas station attendant. He was a young white man. He saw me walking toward him far away, and he turned his head from side to side repeatedly. That was a gesture of telling me that he would not accept my check. I returned to the lawn and sat there.

How can I go home? Only if I had two dollars, I could go home. Cars passing the highway came to the gas station for gas. Should I beg for $2 from them? I got up with the intention of begging and walked to the people who were putting gas in their cars. But when I came close to them face to face, it was impossible for me to say, "Please, give me $2 to buy gas and go home." I returned to the lawn and sat there.

I sat there without any solution. Then I prayed again and was encouraged to go back to the gas station attendant. He saw me coming from far away and moved head from side to side again. I returned to the lawn and sat there.

My mind was getting difficult and bruised. My mind was heavy and difficult not with those who reject my Bible study request and despise me, nor with those who do not move a finger to help but grab benefits in the church.

My mind was heavy and difficult with those who are noble, ideal, and exemplary believers in the church. They always attend Sunday worship service without skipping. They offer tithe without missing. They do their parts assigned to them for church events. Then they enjoy life and have a good time. They eat whatever they want to eat, wear clothes whatever they want to wear, wear shoes whatever they want to wear, they enjoy their hobbies, and vacations. They make money well, buy expensive furniture, cars, and live in luxurious homes, as if they were telling that God blessed them and they were enjoying the blessings.

Why is my life of faith suffering after suffering? Why shouldn't I live my life of faith like them? Couldn't I live a Christian's life like them eating, resting, and enjoying my day off? They save money and are building up their riches, but I am unable to go home because I don't have two dollars to buy gas.

I worked a full time job as a registered nurse, but I had no money saved. I put all my time and money into Bible studies. Once I was out of money and food and skipped one meal. When I went to another city for Bible study, it took 5-8 hours for one Bible study plus money for gas. If I worked 5-8 hours of overtime every week instead of Bible study and saved the money for gas, I would make a fortune.

But I did not calculate overtime money. Bible study is a totally different subject from making money. It is the work of heaven, belonging to heaven. It cannot be calculated or compared with money. When a person receives the word of God and comes to the Lord, I am happy, the angels of heaven are happy, and the Lord is pleased. I poured all my money, time, and life into that. I was convinced that I was doing right and I did it with joy even though there were sufferings on and off.

But that day my mind was bruised by the role model of exemplary Christians. Yet I did not want to follow their lives of faith. Only thinking about their life made me difficult. I could not make any meaningful conclusion. The only conclusion I arrived at was; "I am different."

I spent almost 3-4 hours at the gas station, and I went to the gas station attendant 4-5 times. The sun was touching the horizon of the open field. It would be dark very soon. Again I prayed and walked to the gas station attendant. He saw me coming from far away. This time he did not shake his head from side to side. He accepted my $5 check, I put gas in, and drove home to Toledo.

I am different from them and I will be continuously different from them.

Chapter 10: Fake Missionaries

Fake Missionary #1

I started the church in Toledo, Ohio from my attic room. The rent was $65 a month. The church grew over 15 years, but my husband and I were kicked out of the church because my husband pointed out the corruption of the headquarters. Some time after I visited Korea and gave my testimony at one church about how I pioneered the church in Toledo.

After my testimony, several students came to me and surrounded me. One male college student said to me, "Not long ago xxx missionary gave us his testimony on how he pioneered the church in Toledo. We were so inspired that we prayed loudly to the Lord to give us faith like him."

Next one female student said, "Now, we are very confused. We don't know whose report we should believe. Who really pioneered the church in Toledo?"

I answered simply, "I did." In this world we live in, there are so many fake, copycats which act like authentic; fake bags, fake watches, fake shoes, fake rings, fake certificates of college degrees, fake heirs of rich families, fake beauty.......................in order to live in such a world we have to have discernment to see which is fake and which is authentic. Without discernment, we become a victim of deception. Now I add to the fake items fake missionaries.

Fake Missionary #2

I attended a church conference. While I was listening to one mission report, I felt intuitively that his mission report might be a fake. His mission report consisted of various data and his picture with some native people of his mission field. But he did not say or could not say anything that tells that he was truly involved in mission work.

For example, in another mission report on the same day, the speaker said, "That day the church people slaughtered a cow for meals." This told me that he was really there. Then another person corrected him, "It was not a cow but a pig." He was there, too. The first person saw and knew an animal was slaughtered, but he did not know it was a pig, and the second person knew that a pig was slaughtered instead of a cow because he was there.

In another mission report the speaker showed a picture saying, "It rained heavily that day." But the picture did not show any rain. He could say that because he was there.

I really wanted to know the real identity of the suspicious missionary. After I returned home, I added a new prayer topic to my prayer list.

"Lord, how do you see xxx missionary in your eyes? Let me see him just as You see him."

I prayed for several weeks or months. One day I had a dream. I was in a house basement. Church people were on the first floor. In the basement, there was a water filter system. The church on the first floor received the filtered and purified water from the basement filter system.

The xxx missionary was in the basement. He installed a pipe to the filter system and was stealing the purified water which was supposed to go to the church. No one knew what he was doing. The church people on the first floor were naive. I saw boils in his forearm and body. He was a sick man. He looked miserable and I felt sorry for him. I kept what I saw in my dream to myself. His deception had to be proved through formal investigation and evidence, not through my dream. I saw in my dream that he who gave a mission report was a thief and a sick man.

I mention here about two fake religious men. They were speakers at a conference to hundreds or over a thousand audience and inspired them. This problem of fake religious men existed in the first church and always existed in churches.

Let's look at Revelation chapter 2. The believers of the church in Ephesus had discernment to find out the fake religious men in their church. They tested and exposed the fake apostles. Jesus acknowledged and commended them. (Revelation 2:2)

But the believers of the church in Pergamum were not keen on the presence and activities of the fake religious men in the church. The fake acted like authentic teachers. (Revelation 2:14,15) Jesus asked the believers of the church in Pergamum to repent. Otherwise, Jesus would come and fight against the fake teachers with the sword of His mouth.

The fake copycats of a world work in the world where people deceive others and are deceived. But the fake religious men work in churches which are the holy house of God, and the holy body of Christ. They work with lies and deceptions in church. Sooner or later they will confront Jesus who comes with a sword in His mouth to fight them. If they wish to live one more day longer, they'd better stop lies and deceptions in the church of God.

Chapter 11:
Repentance Of Ministers

A lay believer is a human and a sinner. He has to repent when sinned. A minister is a human and a sinner. He has to repent when sinned. Repenting sin is difficult for everyone, but it is easier for a lay believer to repent than a minister to repent. I learned this through my own experience.

I used to work in a hospital in a dialysis department. I worked closely with dialysis doctors. The doctors came from many different parts of the world, diverse in races and genders; white, African American, Hispanic, Arabic, Asian, men and women. Among them, I noticed one African American doctor was very smart. I always tried to figure out the patient's condition and find out the reason. When the patient's doctor came, I asked about it and listened to the doctor's explanations. Through that I saw that the African American doctor was very smart. I liked smart people. I liked exceptionally smart people.

So I took care of his patients well and paid more attention to his patients. He knew that and he expressed thanks to me. I began to wait for his round and I was joyful when he showed up. This occurred slowly over several months. That's all.

Because of this, my soul was dark, as if dark clouds before rain. I knelt down on my knees, confessed my sins, and asked God's forgiveness. Even after this confession of sins, and I stayed away from the doctor, my soul remained in darkness. There was no coming of the Holy Spirit to burn my sinful heart. Why is it so?

I traced back to my first repentance when I was a beginner believer. I knelt down on my knees and confessed my sins of stealing hospital papers. God accepted my repentance and baptized me with the Holy Spirit. At that time my confession was done in my room alone before God. I did exactly the same way, yet the Lord did not respond to me and my soul remained dark.

In such a struggle I realized that the Lord wanted me to confess my sins before God and church congregation. It was because I was the wife of a pastor and a minister. It was an extremely difficult matter for me to do. What would the church members think about me? Worse than that, what would my husband think about me? Will my marriage break? It was too shameful for me to have an open confession. So I was putting off day by day having an open confession.

I endured hardships well: cold, and hot weather, tiredness, poverty and sorrow..........ect. But it was unbearably painful when my relationship with God was cut off, and my soul remained dark. The suffering was so severe that I couldn't bear any more. I reached the point that nothing mattered to me anymore.

It didn't matter what church members might think and say. It didn't matter what my husband might think and respond. If he wanted to divorce me, then let it be. I didn't care. I had to restore my relationship with God at any cost.

I wrote down my sins in my journal and read it in a small group meeting. Of course, my husband was present at the meeting and was listening to what I was reading. Then something that I had never expected happened.

When I was about to read about my sins, the phone rang. At that time there were no cell phones. All phones were landline phones. The phone rang from another room nearby. My husband got up and left to answer the phone in another room. As soon as I finished the part of confessing my sins, my husband returned and sat in his chair. The timing was precise.

Was the phone call coming by chance or was it done by the Lord? I believed that it was done by the Lord because I had another experience in which the Lord helped me with a phone call.

This time the Lord accepted my repentance and responded. The darkness in my soul was gone. Light began to shine in my soul. Guilty feelings were gone, too.

Through this I learned that the Lord wanted an open repentance before God and church when a minister should repent his sins. Because this was extremely difficult for me, I never, never again sin in my thoughts. When a sinful thought or desire comes into my heart, I make an effort to expel it. I pray until it is removed.

When a minister sins, and the Lord wants an open confession of sins before God and church, his choice is either one, to make an open confession or to refuse to protect his name and honor. If he chooses to protect his name and honor, the sin in him will grow, burst open, and the whole world will know about his sins anyway.

Those who received little will be quired less, and those who received more will be required more. Those who sin without knowledge will be punished less, and those who sin with knowledge will be punished more.

Chapter 12:
People Who Are Curious To Know More About Others Sin

After I confessed my sin in my journal to a small group, a quiet noble missionary came to me. With a gentle smile on his face, he asked me to tell him more about my sins. He was at the small group meeting and heard my confession of my sins. I was flabbergasted. Did he imagine that there should be a more juicy part of the sin that I did not reveal? I ignored him and he deserved it.

Either the same day or a few days later, I don't remember exactly, an intellectual female missionary came to me. With a gentle smile on her face, she politely said that she wanted to know more about my sins. She was also present at the small group meeting and heard my confession. She seemed to have a strong curiosity to know more about the sin of the pastor's wife. It was obvious that she was thinking that there would be more than I revealed. She could not hold her curiosity and came to ask me to speak up to her satisfaction. These people crossed the limit.

Not only these two but also others might have had the curiosity to know more about my sin. But others did not come to ask me because they had a sense of shame about doing it. The above two persons did not have a sense of shame.

Who would confess his/her sins before these shameless people in the church? Who would confess their sins if church listeners reacted in this way trying to satisfy their curiosity? Repentance of confessing sins is disappearing from churches. Churches are changing to a place of socializing, showing their money, cars, houses, the success of their children, and their business. Where should sinners go to be saved from sins?

Once one church member came to me asking me to tell her about a certain brother's sin. Everybody knew about his sin, but she was not satisfied with what she knew and heard. She wanted to know more in detail. I answered her, "If you promise me one thing to do, then I will tell you about the brother's sin. Promise me that you will pray for him every day for months or for years until he is fully restored from his sins." Then she turned around and left. She wanted to know the brother's sin but did not want to take the burden of prayer for his recovery. As a matter of fact, it took 8 years of prayer and the brother was fully restored.

When one sins against another, he sins both against God and the victim because he violated God's truth. Sin does not disappear gradually as time passes. Shame and guilt remain. A sinner needs forgiveness from the victim and God.

In the Old Testament God opened a way of forgiveness for sinners. In Leviticus chapter 4 there are four groups of sinners; an anointed priest, the whole nation, a leader of society, and a commoner.

There was a common factor in the offering of sin offerings to God even though the animals of sin offering and some details were different according to each group.

Sin offerings were offered to God in the temple in Jerusalem in the presence of God. A sinner who wanted to be forgiven brought an animal as a sin offering to the temple. This animal was called a sacrificial animal. The animal was tied up on a table so that it couldn't move. The sinner placed his hand on the head of the animal and confessed his sins. Then the sin transferred to the animal. The animal became an animal of sin. The animal had to die because of sin in it by the hand of the man who gave it his sins. The sinner held a sharp tool and stabbed a vital part of the immobilized animal. The animal bled and was dying.

Then the attending priest collected the running and dripping blood of the animal and offered the blood before God as prescribed, interceding between God and a sinner for the forgiveness of sins.

> "............In this way the priest will make atonement for them, and they will be forgiven."
>
> Leviticus 4:20

> "............ In this way the priest will make atonement for the man's sin, and he will be forgiven.
>
> Leviticus 4:26

> "............In this way the priest will make atonement for him, and he will be forgiven.
>
> Leviticus 4:31

"..............In this way the priest will make atonement for him for the sin he has committed, and he will be forgiven.

Leviticus 4:35

The temple was destroyed by fire in AD70. Yet God's forgiveness continues to all who sinned. Jesus is the sin offering in place of animal offerings. Jesus is tied up on the cross so that he couldn't move. We put our hand on the head of Jesus and confess our sins. Our sin goes to Jesus. Jesus becomes a sinner because of the sins we gave him. Jesus must bleed and die on the cross. God accepts the blood of Jesus and forgives us.

"Look, the Lamb of God, who takes away the sin of the world!" John 1:29

But God wants confession of sins from the mouth of the sinner. When I confessed my sin for the first time, I was alone in a room before God. God accepted the confession and baptized me with the Holy Spirit. After I became a servant of the Lord and my position in the church was significant, the Lord wanted me to confess my sins before God and church.

When I wrote about my sin and read in a small group was a part of the process of sin offering. It was a holy ceremony to receive the forgiveness of God. People who were at the small group meeting were the witnesses of my confession and God's forgiveness.

Should they come back and ask me to explain more about my sins in detail? Something is wrong with them.

Chapter 13: Prayer Has Its End

Some prayers are answered right away, but some prayers are answered after several months or years. But always prayer has an end. The end of prayer comes when God finally answers the prayer.

Our problem is giving up prayers. After several times of praying, we quit. After several days of prayer, we quit again saying it is no use to pray. Then we seek a solution in our own human ways. God will decide whether to answer or not to these short-lived prayers or quit prayers.

What I want to say is that prayer has its end. That's why I pray until I see the ending of prayer. When I see the ending, then I stop the specific prayer. Once we start to pray with one specific prayer topic, we should pray to the end no matter how long it may take; 10 years, 20 years, or 30 years. Isaac prayed for 20 years for his wife Rebekah who was barren. After 20 years of prayer, God answered his prayer and gave her twin boys. (Genesis 25:19,26)

There was a church conference in Galveston, Texas. There was a deck in Galveston beach and a hotel on the deck. The conference took place at the hotel. About 35-40 missionaries attended the conference and I was in charge of preparing meals. When I was preparing a meal, one missionary came to me saying that he was on a vegetarian diet due to his poor health. He would eat only vegetarian food.

It was the first time I met him. I did not know his name or where he was living. His face was very pale and I felt sorry for him because his pale face was compared with the healthy complexion of other missionaries.

When the conference was over, I decided to pray for him until he recovered his health. I didn't see any meaning of our growth when one person drops and falls behind. We should help him recover from his illness and we should move forward together. For that reason, his recovery was more important than the whole ministry. I will go forward with the sick missionary in my heart. In fact, when I prayed for him, with my arms I was holding him in my imagination, rubbing over his sick area with my imaginary hand.

In the beginning, I prayed for his healing three times a day, then twice a day, then once a day. He had 6 or 7 sicknesses in his body from head to toe, and I had never seen a person who had so many illnesses in one body. He was carried to the emergency room once in a while because of severe pain.

I said to one missionary that I pray for his healing. He answered me, "Don't pray for him. He has too many problems." I thought that was the general opinion about him across the church. They have given up on him because he had too many problems. The God I believe is Almighty God. Everything is possible with God. I didn't mind many of his problems. I kept on praying for his healing.

Maybe about ten years have passed. I lived in Houston and he lived in another state. I could see him once or twice a year at the conference. When I did not hear about his sickness, I assumed that he might have been healed and stopped praying. But later I heard from his wife that his condition became worse and I resumed my prayers once a day. What I did not understand was the more I prayed, the worse his condition was. Despite his worsening condition I kept on praying for him. Then the end of the prayer arrived. It took 15 years in all.

One day I was talking with one of our church members. He came from Korea with his wife recently. He was a chiropractor. He talked to me about how he cured some sick patients. I said to him that there was such a sick missionary with such, such illnesses. I asked him;

"Can you heal him?" He answered, "Yes."

I said, "Then go to him in North Carolina right away."

The chiropractor Kim said that he had to go with his wife. That meant two round flight tickets instead of one. In order to cut expenses I suggested bringing the sick missionary to Houston and treating him in Houston. The chiropractor Kim opposed the suggestion. He might not be able to cure the sick man when his mind is uncomfortable and disturbed by staying at other's homes. The best optimal condition for healing the sick man would be at his own home with his wife helping beside him. A Peaceful and comfortable mind is essential for healing.

I answered, "Very well. Leave soon to North Carolina with your wife."

Afterwards, he said again that he had to take the metal massage table with him. The delivery fee was not cheap. I answered, "Very well. We will pay the air delivery fee for the massage table."

All these expenses were paid with a church account and the church coworkers paid these expenses with joyful hearts. Chiropractor Kim said that he needed at least 3 months to heal him due to his serious conditions but he had only a little over one month free time from his school.

So he bought two round tickets for just a little over one month.

I called the sick missionary's home to notify the arrival of chiropractor Kim and his wife. The patient's wife answered the phone. She said that her husband might die if he does not heal this time. He was very, very sick. He had been sick for 15 more years since I had started praying for him.

I respect her whenever I see her. Other men have good jobs and bring home money. She cares for her husband who has been getting sicker and sicker every year for the last 15 years.

She dearly loves her sick husband and manages her family life. I felt respect and greatness from her. 5 or 6 days passed since chiropractor Kim, his wife, and the massage table left for North Carolina. I received a phone call from chiropractor Kim;

"Last night xxx missionary slept without taking any pills."

The sick missionary had insomnia. He could not sleep with two sleeping pills prescribed by his doctor. He added a couple of more sedatives in addition to the prescribed sleeping pills. Just 5-6 days after the arrival of chiropractor Kim, and began his treatment, the patient went to sleep without any pills.

Beginning with this news I heard everyday victory news of healing one after another. The illnesses he had for the last 10-15 years were cured one by one probably in 10 days or less than two weeks. Chiropractor Kim himself was surprised by the miraculous healing. Chiropractor Kim and his wife went outside and talked about this unexpected miraculous healing. He said to his wife; "This is a miracle. It is not I who healed him."

When chiropractor Kim and his wife returned to Houston after being used by God, we went to the airport with flowers. It was a day of great joy and victory. God ended 15 years of prayers with joy and miracles. Lord, we love you!

Later I could hear about the healing in detail from chiropractor Kim. The way of his healing was basically establishing a healthy lifestyle and providing nutritious meals. At the same time, he approached the patient's sickness one by one. Eating well, pooping well, and sleeping well in a peaceful mind is the foundation of healing and a healthy life.

In order to establish a healthy life the chiropractor Kim did everything together 24/7 with his patient. They got up at 6 am together, jogged together, ate breakfast together, rested together, exercised together, and went to bed at the same time. There was no nap in their daily schedule.

Mrs. Kim, the wife of chiropractor Kim, managed the nutritional needs. She made a daily menu with all natural foods and vitamins. The Patient's wife cooked meals according to the menu and served all of them.

Chiropractor Kim explained to me how he approached his patient's insomnia. He saw that his patient kept an alarm clock closely and always calculated how long he slept. The alarm clock was there to help his sleep but chiropractor Kim saw the adverse effect on the patient's mind by distracting him. So chiropractor Kim first removed the alarm clock from his patient. This reminded me of what he said to me in the past. "I do everything to heal my patient. When it does not work, I enter the inside of the patient's mind."

The next night chiropractor Kim put the four pills that the patient usually took for sleep and said to his patient, "Remove one pill and take the rest. Let's try to sleep tonight with three pills." That night the patient slept well with three pills. He might have been tired of the new daily schedule. The next night the pills were reduced to two pills and the patient slept well with two pills. The next night the pills were reduced to one pill, and he slept well. Finally, the patient slept without taking any pills, and he slept well.

By that time chiropractor Kim worried about possible withdrawal symptoms as he proceeded like this. Sleeping pills and sedatives should be tapered down and tapered off very slowly over a period of 1-2 months to prevent from body's withdrawal symptoms. Chiropractor Kim removed four pills in four days. Withdrawal symptoms might occur. But a miracle happened. No withdrawal symptoms occurred. The Patient slept well without any pills ever since. God intervened and helped in this matter. This cannot be explained with medical knowledge, but in the world of prayer, everything is possible. After several weeks the fully recovered missionary participated in the 5K marathon and was running.

God answers some prayers right away and our problems are solved right away. But some prayers are not answered after weeks and months, and we face a long prolonged frustration.

The situation when we start to pray in the beginning is a struggle between me and my problem. In order to overcome a problem we go to God in prayer.

I vs my problem

But when time passes and my prayer is not answered, prayer enters a new phase, a long-term phase. My problem will be pushed aside, and the match will be between God and me. The position of God may be 'Let's see how long you keep your faith in prayer.' My position will be, 'Lord, I never quit. I pray to the end.' So the match is;

I vs God

Jesus explained this match through the parable of a persistent widow and a judge in Luke 18:1-8. In this parable Jesus did not mention the problems of the widow. We don't know about her enemy and what her enemy did to her. That was not the key to her solution. The key to resolving her problem was the match between the judge and her. She had to win the match with the judge. It was a match between her persistence and the stubborn judge who neither feared God nor cared about men. This tells that it is not easy to move the mind of the judge.

Is this a match of a century? Who would win? The persistence of the widow won over the stubbornness of the judge. The judge surrendered to her and accepted her case. This is the exact same situation when our prayer enters into a long phase. We are in a match with God. We have to win this match. We have to pray to the end until God surrenders through our relentless, persistent prayers. We have to make God tired and surrender as the widow did. That day when God answers our prayers is a day of great joy, a day of victory, and a day of miracles. Jesus ended this parable in Luke 18:8 by saying; "However, when the Son of Man comes, will he find faith on the earth?"

Chapter 14:
The End Of The Age

There was the beginning of this world, and there will be the end of this world. This world is in progress toward the end.

No one knows about that day or hour. God put the time of the end under His authority. "No one knows about that day or hour, not even the angels in heaven nor the Son but only the Father." (Matthew 24:36, Mark 13:32)

About the day what the angels do not know, what Jesus does not know, a human being proclaims, "I know the day!" When I was in elementary school, one church proclaimed, "We know the day! In August 1986, Jesus will come!" It was the early 1960's and the year 1986 was a future of more than 25 years. People flocked to that church like a gathering of clouds.

I decided to wait and watch. That day came and nothing happened.

This kind of claim happened many times in the past, it is happening at present time, and it will happen in the future. People who are smarter than angels, smarter than Jesus appear and disappear after predicting the last day and collecting some money. If you hear any individual or group predicting the last day, run away from them as soon as possible. There is something wrong when people know more than Jesus.

Jesus may come today or after a week or a month or after many years. Jesus who watches everything happening in this world, will decide; 'I will go to my children who are in the world.' That moment Jesus will come. We wait for that moment while doing our jobs and keeping our faith. The moment comes suddenly when we do not expect it. (Matthew 24:44, Mark 13:36, Luke 12:40)

Had Jesus known the day or the hour, Jesus would have told his disciples. But He said that He did not know. But Jesus taught the disciples about what He knew, about the process or the pattern of coming to the end of the age.

"These are the beginning of birth pains." (Matthew 24:8, Mark 13:8) Jesus compares the process of the coming of the end with birth pain. Men would not know the progress of birth pains. But mothers who delivered babies know very well.

Labor pains come slowly and endurably. Mom knows that the labor pain has begun. As time passes, it comes more frequently with stronger pains. Mom rests between pains but the pain intensifies and comes in shorter intervals.

The process of the coming of the end times is similar. The disaster comes slowly at the beginning but increases in frequency and intensity. The disasters are earthquakes and famines as mentioned in Matthew 24:9, and Mark 13:7.

We have been already living in this process of the end times. Compare the disasters of this year with those of last year. Have the disasters been lessened or intensified? Have the floods and the heat been decreased or increased?

In Houston, we had a month long triple digit heat. I hear more people saying, "It is the end of the ages." Look at the sick people; drug addicts, mentally ill people, cancer patients. Are the number of sick people decreasing or increasing? Why does the number of sick children increase? Children 30-40 years ago were healthier.

Next year will be more difficult to live than this year because the frequency and the severity of disasters will intensify like labor pain.

Jesus said, "Now, learn this lesson from the fig tree. As soon as its twigs get tender and its leaves come out, you know that summer is near." (Matthew 24:32) In early spring green tender shoots show up here and there in a fig tree. People can guess that summer is on the way.

People know the time of the near future. To know the time of the near future is not difficult. It does not require research or study. Common sense is enough to know the time of the near future.

To know the time of the end of the ages is as simple as this fig tree. Jesus already taught the signs and symptoms of the end times, which can be used as indications as the tender green shoots of a fig tree. They are all written in Daniel, Matthew chapter 24, Mark chapter 13, Luke chapter 21, and Revelation.

When we see the signs and symptoms written in these occurring in real life, we can tell the time of the near future. I knew a damaging flood was coming. It is written in Luke

21:25. I knew unprecedented heat would come. It is written in Revelation 16:8,9.

Jesus said to the crowd, "When you see a cloud rising in the west, immediately you say, 'It's going to rain,' and it does. (Luke 12:54) Even little children know this. My grandson who was 3 or 4 years old was playing in my backyard. He came to me saying, "Grandma, dark clouds are coming in the sky. It looks like it is going to rain. Let's go inside."

Concerning the end times, I divide people into two groups; one group of people who know the time, and the other group who do not know the time. Those who see the clouds' coming know that the rain is coming soon like my grandson did, and would stop what they are doing and prepare to avoid the rain. They would prepare an umbrella or cancel outdoor events or move a parked car from a low place to a higher place. But those who see the clouds coming, and do not know that the rain is coming, they would get wet in the rain or hit by lightning or be swept by torrent of flood. Some may lose life. They are not prepared because they do not know the time.

What do multiple forest fires tell about a time of the near future? What does the three months long unprecedented heat tell about a time of the near future? What do the floods that covered fields, villages, and cities predict in the near future?

The answer is obvious. Famine is on the way in the near future. There will be no harvest when grains dry up and die by heat, no harvest when floods sweep over farms and fields. What should people prepare when they know that famine is on the way? People prepare foods and water, foods that will last months and years. People who prepare will suffer less.

But those who see unprecedented heat and floods, who cannot interpret the coming time, do not prepare anything. When food prices jump up 10 times, 20 times or even cannot be bought with money or gold, then they realize, 'Ah, famine is here.' Some are proud of themselves for not knowing the time through signs. They think that they are not swayed by rumors and theories of the end times.

When Jesus taught about the end of the age, He began with these words;

"Watch out that no one deceives you." (Matthews 24:4)

We need to interpret time through signs. We also need to be careful not to be deceived. These two instructions combined tell; watch out, be awake.

So I would like to talk about deceptions. Deception is the nature of the devil. Deception of the devil is like fishing with a fishing hook. Each fish has a favorite bate it likes. The Fisherman hides a hook through a bait and throws the hook into the water. Fish does not see the hidden hook but only sees the bait and bites the bait. The joyful time of eating the bait is very short. The fish is dragged by the fishing line and dies.

At the end of the age, deceptions are widespread like the air in the sky, like the waters in the ocean. That's why Jesus taught, "Watch out that no one deceives you," Sweet deceptions are all around us.

Years ago there was a popular song among young Americans. It was a song praising Lucifer (the name of Satan). I did not hear the song but I knew the existence of the song. So I asked a teenager in our church about it. He said that he ignored the lyrics but listened to the music because the music was good. He worshiped the Lord in the church and enjoyed such music later. He was deceived when he followed the trend. That was a bit of music.

There are many other bates. Businessmen want money. Scholars want knowledge. Politicians want power. Scientists want inventions. Actors want success and popularity. Artists want artistic inspiration. Some want physical pleasures. Unemployed men want jobs. The Devil knows what each person wants. The Devil puts bait on a hook and waits until one comes and bites the bait with willingness and a voluntary decision. The devil has all the kingdoms of the world and their splendor (Matthew 4:8) and promises success, money, and whatever people want. The joy of biting the bait is short. The person who is deceived is dragged by the fishing line.

In this age, deception is wide-spread. Many baits are placed here and there waiting for people to bite it. Free seminars, new apartment sales, 70% sale, new ideas, a famous person.........we should not bite it quickly. We must pray to the Lord, and ask;

"Lord, should I buy this or not?"

"Lord, should I meet this person or not?"

"Lord, should I go to this concert or not?"

I pray when I go to a grocery store. "Lord, should I go to this grocery store or that grocery store?" Inside of a store, a man came to me and asked me to give him money. In another store, a man followed me. I asked a cashier to escort me to my car. But he was too busy with many customers. I had to be on my own. I outwitted the stalker and returned home safely. For my own safety I ask the Lord. The Lord knows which way I should go and be safe, but I don't know. I have no insight to see a hidden hook beneath a bait, but God knows a hidden hook.

"If anyone of you lacks wisdom, he should ask God, who gives generously to all without finding fault, and it will be given to him." James 1:5

I read this passage first before I ask the Lord very stupid questions. The Lord never rebuked me for asking Him stupid questions. He answers me kindly. Shall I go to this grocery or that grocery? Shall I drive on the expressway or local ways? Shall I give this bread to this family or to that family?

In the end times, there will be persecution against Christians as the disasters intensify its frequency and severity. Believers in Jesus will face a situation to choose either one; deny Jesus and live or keep faith in Jesus and die. We have freedom of religion. But the day will come when people lose that freedom.

The freedom of religion is protected by the Constitution. How will it be possible to lose the freedom of religion? I thought about it and one day I found the answer. When martial law is proclaimed, the martial law will be effective new laws and the Constitution will cease.

Jesus said, "For whoever wants to save his life will lose it, but whoever loses his life for me will find it." Matthew 16:25

What should I choose? Should I deny Jesus to live longer and lose eternal life? Or should I keep my faith in Jesus and be killed but have eternal life? It is better to think about it now while we have enough time to think, decide, and prepare our hearts. If we are not prepared, there is a high possibility of denying Jesus driven by fear. Jesus said,

"At that time many will turn away from the faith and will betray and hate each other." (Matthew 24:9,10)

During the Japanese occupation of Korea, the Japanese demanded Koreans to worship the Japanese emperor. Our grandfathers faced the situation of worshiping the Japanese emperor as god. Many believers bowed down before the picture of the emperor in order to live. Those who refused and kept their faith in Jesus were arrested and put into prisons. I don't know what happened to them in the prison.

I studied the Bible with one brother who came from Congo, Africa. His village was suddenly attacked by soldiers, and the whole village became hostages. The soldiers put all the village people in one line. They placed a cross on the ground. Anyone who stepped on the cross was allowed to live. Anyone who walked around the cross was shot to death on the spot. The brother was a believer in Jesus. But he stepped on the cross and was allowed to live. He stepped on the cross because he was so scared and terrified.

"But he who stands firm to the end will be saved."

(Matthew 24:13)

I collected passages about the coming of Jesus.

There will be signs in the sun, moon, and stars............ At that time they will see the Son of Man coming in a cloud with power and great glory."

(Luke 21:25,27)

But in those days following that distress,

"The sun will be darkened, and the moon will not give its light;

The stars will fall from the sky, and the heavenly bodies will be shaken."

At that time men will see the Son of Man coming in clouds with great power and glory.

(Mark 13:24,25,26)

"..............That is how it will be in the field; one will be taken and the other left."

(Matthew 24:39,40)

"Two women will be grinding with a hand mill; one will be taken and the other left."

(Matthew 24:41, Luke 17:35)

"I tell you, on that night two people will be in one bed; one will be taken and the other left."

(Luke 17:34)

I found something strange in these passages. All of them describe the coming of Jesus, but the backgrounds are different. One background was cosmic chaos. Another background was peaceful ordinary life.

Will two men work in the field when the sun turns to darkness and stars fall from the sky? No. they won't. They would be terrified. Will two women be grinding with a hand mill to prepare food when the sun turns to darkness and the stars fall from sky? No. They would be scared and hide inside their homes. These two different backgrounds cannot be compromised as one event. So I concluded that Jesus comes twice; once on a peaceful ordinary day, and the next during cosmic chaos. But I prayed to the Lord; "Lord, the backgrounds of Jesus' coming are different. One background is peaceful ordinary life and the other background is cosmic chaos. I must know about it. I don't want to teach something wrong and inaccurate. I can teach accurately when I know the real meaning. Teach me why there are two different backgrounds."

I kept on praying like this and after about 3 weeks I had a dream about a rapture. Jesus' coming on a peaceful ordinary day is rapture. Jesus' coming during cosmic chaos is Jesus' second coming at the end of this world. Both rapture and Jesus' second coming are about Jesus' coming, but they are two different events.

The rapture is an event that Jesus comes to take His people out of this world. The rapture will take place at the same time throughout the whole world. So one side of the earth is day, and the opposite side of the earth is night.

Day - two men in the field, two women are grinding.

Night - on that night two people will be in one bed

When one is lifted, he is taken at a speed faster than light. It is too fast and it is impossible to see in human eyes. It is like it has just gone. The other person left behind thinks, 'Oh? Where is he? He was in front of me.' But he does not realize that the rapture occurred at that moment right in front of his eyes.

When two women are grinding with a hand mill, they are sitting closely together almost side by side. One woman just disappears. One second is too long a time. It may be 1/1000 of a second. The remaining woman cannot see the lifting of the other woman even though she has kept her eyes open. It is too fast to see with human eyes. The remaining woman knows that one woman is gone but does not realize that the rapture has taken place.

In my dream, I was in a small church attending a worship service. There were about a dozen people. One in front of me was gone while I had my eyes open. I was not lifted and remained. I vaguely began to realize that the rapture had taken place. The rest of the church members did not know that the rapture had taken place minutes ago. They had no idea about rapture. They continued routine casual church life as usual. The Rapture occurs like lightning on a quiet ordinary day. People are not aware of it and continue their usual activities. But later they know because many people are gone.

Jesus' second coming is different from rapture. The sun will be darkened and the moon will not give its light and the stars will fall from the sky. The whole world would be very dark. Then suddenly the sky will be brightened with light and trumpet sound. All peoples on earth will see Jesus' coming in a cloud with power and great glory. People are terrified and hide at the scene because they know that judgment is at hand. But the believers who have waited for that moment enduring all kinds of sufferings will lift up their heads. Everyone on earth will see and know this event.

For the people who live in the end times the best choice is to prepare for the rapture. Rapture is the amazing God's love and care for the people living in end times.

How should one prepare for the rapture? Please, read Matthew 24:42-51 and the whole chapter 25. If there is any part you don't understand, ask God and learn from God directly. God understands each person very well, and God knows how to answer our questions. Learning from God for one minute is far greater than learning from another human for ten years. No one knows that I had a chicken as my pet. Once God used chickens to explain to me in my dream, because God knew that using chicken I could understand very well. God is an amazing teacher.

I chose Matthew 24:42-51 as I wait for rapture. I tried to live as a faithful and wise servant. In this parable, the food is the word of God. I identified myself as a servant who feeds the household of God. I taught the words of God every Wednesday, every Thursday, every Friday and gave Sunday messages every other Sunday. For about ten years I did not have a vacation even one day. When Jesus comes, I want to be found as a faithful and wise servant. I threw away a lot of stuff minimizing my living and I had my will prepared.

Those who remain behind in the world after the rapture have to live under the rule of the antichrist. Antichrist does not mean one who is against Christ. It means another

Christ. In other word, 'Jesus did not save you. Follow me, and I will save you.'

People were disappointed with political leaders. Political leaders failed and disappointed people one by one. Still, people think and hope that one good political leader would turn around their lives. So people welcome the antichrist with excitement and expectations believing that their living conditions would improve and live better if they follow him. For that reason, I think the antichrist is a politician. (Revelation 13:1-10) A religious leader is a collaborator with the antichrist. (Revelation 13:11-18). He will force everyone to receive a mark on his right hand or on his forehead. He who receives the mark will be separated from God permanently. (Revelation 13:16, 14:9,10,11, 16:2) Remember this before you receive anything in your right hand.

Antichrist grabs the power and rules the world for 7 years. (the book of Daniel) The last three and a half years is called 'the great tribulation' which is the climax of all sufferings and disasters.

Jesus describes the period; "For then there will be great distress, unequaled from the beginning of the world until now - and never to be equaled again." (Matthew 24:21) The scale of disaster is far beyond human imagination. That's why Jesus gathers His children through rapture before the great tribulation. Believers who are left behind after the rapture must wait for the second coming of Jesus and go through the tribulation. It is going to be an unprecedented disaster after another unprecedented disaster. But when they hold on to salvation in Jesus more than their own life, they also receive salvation and the reward of heaven.

At the end of the great tribulation, Jesus comes in a cloud with power and great glory. The antichrist who was destroying the earth and humanity is captured and killed. The tribulation ends. God makes new heavens, new earth, and new Jerusalem. (Revelation 21) Jesus establishes His kingdom and rules for a thousand years.

Chapter 15:
Banana Bread

In our church, we had a fellowship with snacks after Sunday worship service. Each family rotated and prepared the snacks. When it was my turn to prepare the snack, I always prepared the rice cakes because it was simple and saved time for me. On Saturday I called the rice cake factory and ordered on the phone. The next morning, Sunday morning, I picked the prepared rice cakes from the factory.

I ordered the same kind of rice cakes. One day the factory introduced a new rice cake, a yellow pumpkin rice cake and I bought it for the first time. After the Sunday worship service when we shared the rice cakes, I carefully watched to see whether they liked the new pumpkin rice cake or not. I saw one teenage boy throwing a whole piece of pumpkin rice cake into a trash can.

I thought, "Oh, no! What is he doing? Throwing the pumpkin rice cake into a trash can? He shouldn't do that. I paid money to prepare it." I was thinking what I should do with this matter so that it won't happen again.

The easiest and fastest way was to tell his mom so that his mom might instruct him not to do it again. But I was hesitant to do it because the boy was very careful of his words and actions. I respected his attitude and I did not want to report this to his mom.

I decided to think further and try to find a better solution. He was born and grew up in America. He grew up eating bread and cakes. I was born in Korea eating rice cakes. In his perspective, I was demanding him to enjoy rice cake which he didn't care for but I liked it. If I truly wanted to serve him, I should have served him with bread and cakes which he liked, not what I liked. I found my self-centered attitude. I realized that I should first be changed before I educate the boy. So I decided to learn how to make bread and cakes.

First, I started from the very basics of making bread with yeast. I watched videos from YouTube on how to make bread. After making several loaves of bread using yeast, I moved to making bread using baking powder and baking soda. Next I made castella and red bean bread. Next I alternated red bean bread and banana bread. Both of them were popular.

Then I chose to specialize in banana bread. Red bean bread takes at least four hours to make it while banana bread takes two hours to make. Some people like red bean bread and some don't like it while everyone likes banana bread.

The recipe for banana bread was very basic. With the very basic recipe I began to develop my own ways. I experimented, researched, and tested to improve the taste. Sometimes I baked successfully and sometimes I failed. But my friend says that she welcomes even failed banana bread from me.

Lately I bake banana bread every two weeks. There are two groups of church families nearby, I deliver banana bread to one group and after two weeks I deliver banana bread to another group. Each family receives it once a month even though I bake every two weeks. One American woman who tasted my banana bread commended it as the best banana bread she had ever tasted in her life. I have become an expert in banana bread. The incident of throwing rice cakes led me to be an expert on banana bread. Above all I am serving the teenage boy with what he likes, not what I like.

Chapter 16:
Love For The Succulents

After retirement, I began to grow succulents in my backyard. It was my first time growing succulents. I studied diligently through YouTube and Google. There was always something I could learn from both the experts and the beginners. I also searched for growing succulents in other countries besides America. I watched and read about anything about succulents. I did not want to miss even one single piece of knowledge. Now I don't watch any videos about succulents. My basic study is over.

One video on YouTube had the title of 'Rare Korean Succulents Sale.' I clicked on it. One Philippine woman was selling them, and another Philippine woman who went there to buy them recorded the video.

It was a long video about 25-30 minutes long. Very expensive, high-priced Korean succulents were on display. Some could be 10-20 years old and worth hundreds of dollars or even a thousand dollars in value. The presenter of the video showed them one by one but did not give any comments. After showing all the succulents on shelves, she showed succulents on the ground in a narrow alley. Then there were a lot more in the backyard. Some pots were standing upright, some fell to the sides on the ground. Some looked healthy and some were dying. All the pots, small and big, were made or designed as ceramic pots.

I saw the love for the succulents of the previous owner and the dying, neglected ones in the hand of the present owner. Those were a lot of succulents for one person to take care of, but it was not a farm. It was a private home.

What happened to the previous owner? Was he sick suddenly, hospitalized, and never returned home? Or did he die unexpectedly? Could he have ever imagined that this would happen to his succulents? He might not. Yet this happened to his succulents.

When I looked at the collections of succulents and the pots, I thought that he might be a Korean who lived in the Philippines or a Korean who lived in America. Or he could be a Filipino specializing in Korean succulents. But Philipinos don't pour so much money on succulents, but Koreans do. So it was possible that the previous owner was Korean.

Through this, I thought about my own situation. If I become sick suddenly and stay in a hospital for a long time, what would happen to my lovely babies (my succulents)? What if I suddenly die? My babies (my succulents) would face the same situation. The previous owner neither expected nor prepared for this sad situation.

He got up in the morning and checked his succulents one by one, very expensive rare succulents. He watered them and gave them fertilizer. When he saw a succulent, he just knew what he should do, whether to change the soil, put it in the shade, or put it in the sun. When the succulents displayed colors, he was mesmerized by the beauty of it. But alas! He had to depart and never return.

The same can happen to me and my succulents. The same will happen to me and my succulents. Someday, I will fall. I learned a lesson from him. I and my babies decided to be succulents of blessings, joy, and comfort to others. I began to make succulent arrangements and give to others as a gift. I and my succulents started to spread joy and comfort to others.

So beautiful succulent arrangements began to leave home to give joy and comfort to others.

After several months, I retrieved one succulent arrangement back to me. Some withered or were dying. I welcomed them all back home. "Welcome home! You have done a great job. People were comforted by you. I will put you among your friends.' Other succulents at home were healthy and strong. I said to them, "Welcome your friends who just returned home. Don't bully them." I washed the pot, filled it with a new soil mix, made another arrangement, and sent it out. It is a refill.

One succulent arrangement pot returned home. There were fungus infestations in plants, in soil, and in the pot. I threw away plants and the soil. I wiped the pot with Clorox wipes. I was not convinced that all fungus died. I soaked the pot in Clorox solution for over an hour. Then I cleansed again with soap and a soapy sponge. After I rinsed with water, I was satisfied with the pot. The pot was super clean.

I filled the pot with a new soil mix. I began to start arranging it, thinking about the person who would receive it. I finished the arrangement but I was not content with it. So I prayed, "Lord, this person works so hard to raise her children. I want her to receive rest and comfort from these succulents when she is tired and exhausted. But this arrangement doesn't seem to give her rest and comfort. It should be more beautiful. I could do this far with my own artistic talent. Lord, give me Your artistic talent so that I may make it more beautiful."

After prayer, I made a little change. I prayed again, and I made another change. Prayed again, with more changes. Finally, I was satisfied with the arrangement. I was so tired and I had to go inside to lie down.

When a moment of sudden departure comes to me and to my succulents, I and my succulents won't be in shock. We have been giving joy and comfort to our tired friends.

Chapter 17:
God is love

The fungus infested pot was completely born again after I washed it repeatedly and filled it with new soil mixes and new succulents. It was not recognizable of the withered and dying old shape. The pot was full of vibrant color, beauty, and life.

Then I remembered Jesus. Jesus did the same to us. We were sick and dying. Jesus brought us to Him. He washed, washed, and washed us with His blood until we became clean. He gave us a new heart and adorned us beautifully with the words of God and the Holy Spirit.

The reason why Jesus did it to us was neither we were good, nor were we bad. Jesus did it because of His love in His heart. Because of love in Him He wanted to do it. Jesus shed His blood to make us clean because He wanted. Jesus pulled us closer to Him because He wanted. Then Jesus was pleased in doing it.

I understood this through my love for succulents. Love in my heart was the source of all my activities in my backyard with the succulents. I had to endure the heat in the backyard to take care of them, and despite the heat I was willing to care for them. I had to visit a doctor because I had heat rashes. I did not eat out at a restaurant even once a year to save money and use it for succulents to buy small rocks, soil mixes, all different sizes of pots, and new kinds of succulents at a nursery or in mail order. Love in my heart was the source of all my activities.

Then I realized that the core of all God's activities is love in His heart. The love of God is the first cause of all existence and changes. The love of God is the first cause of creation. The love of God is the first cause of His Sovereignty over the ever changing world. Wow! This was an eye opening discovery while I took care of the succulents. Up until that time the direction of my understanding of God was from me to God, or from someone to God. Now the direction was reversed. I began to see myself from God's love, and the world from God's love. I opened the Bible and read;

"In the beginning God created the heavens and the earth," What did God see? "Now the earth was formless and empty, darkness was over the surface of the deep."

God saw the darkness covered earth with the eyes of love. With love in His heart God wanted to do something good and beautiful. God created for six days and He looked at all His creatures with the eyes of love.

I have the same love in my heart toward the succulents. I look at them with love. Some are healthy, some are eaten by worms, and some are crowded with small babies. I want to do something good for them and I do it using my time and money. I look at them with eyes of love and I am happy after my work is done. I learned that God of creation is God Almighty and I taught like that. Now I realized that God of creation is God of love. God is love. (1John 4:8) God created the world out of His love and governs the world with His love. From the first page of the Bible to the last page of the Bible the love of God flows.

God is love. I knew that in my head as knowledge. The knowledge came into my heart. I wanted to go deeper into the love of God. So I began to meditate on the love of God.

God's love is pure.

It is almost impossible to see purity in people. I see purity in newborn babies. I see purity in flowers. Every year, every month, every day the world is turning to be weirder, and weirder, shocker, and shocker away from purity.

Even though everything is corrupt when a man and a woman start to love each other, they want pure love. It is like; let the world be corrupt, but let my love be pure. Why do people want their love pure? Is it people's last wish in this world? But they find corrupted love. Love without purity is not love but a conditional love with a calculator calculating gain and loss. Humans have limits of money, time, health, physical looks, and life which, I think, changes pure love to conditional love with a calculator.

God does not have any limits. God can love unconditionally and forever. There is no calculator in God's love. Such love is the love of God. God's love remains pure forever. My love for God may turn conditional but God's love for me remains pure forever. Therefore I have fallen in God's love and I do not regret it. I am happy when I meditate on God's love every morning. Mentioned about purity Jesus said, "Blessed are the pure in heart, for they will see God." Matthew 5:8

People see or perceive through the eyes of the heart. Crooks see an opportunity to deceive others while ordinary people do not see. Thieves see an opportunity to steal while others do not see. Sex offenders see what they want to see. Dirty hearts see dirty things and impure hearts see impure things. Pure hearts see pure things and they will see God.

God's love is holy.

Purity and holiness are different words and have different meanings. During Bible study my Bible student asked me; what is holiness? I couldn't answer. It is something that people learn the meaning through experiencing it. It is impossible to learn by watching with eyes or hearing through ears. It can not be explained in words. Although I can not explain in words there is holiness.

When the Holy Spirit comes into our hearts and touches our hearts, then we experience holiness. Holiness is one of God's attributes which only God has. God's love is holy.

God's love is beautiful.

God revealed the beauty of His love through His creation. The whole creation is God's art work. Artistic people capture the beauty of nature in paintings, photographs, and designs. Before the creation, the earth was empty, formless, and dark. Through creation, God brought colors, lines, angles, shapes, textures, and designs by mixing them. What an amazing artist God is. When I look at a flower, I stand in front of it for 10 or 20 or 30 minutes, mesmerized by its beauty of colors, shape, and design. These are beauties we can appreciate with our eyes.

There is also invisible spiritual beauty. Rahab in Jericho was a prostitute. (Joshua 2:1) Such a woman can not come to our church because of shame. Church members find out about her job and talk about it day and night. This Rahab joined the genealogy of Jesus and she became a great, great, grandmother of king David. (Matthew 1:5)

As a prostitute, she had frequent contacts with travelers and foreigners. She was keenly aware of the news about what was going on in neighboring kingdoms. Israel was invading neighboring kingdoms, and had victory after victory. She knew that the God of Israel was the true God among all gods. She knew what God did in the past, what God is doing now, and what God will do in the future. Israel was preparing to invade her own country Jericho. She chose God of Israel, instead of her own nation. Her knowledge about God outshined the darkness of her past life. This is invisible spiritual beauty. I met many women like Rahab. They were beautiful.

God makes everything beautiful.

God's love is resurrection.

When I grow succulents, I don't throw away anything that is not dead. I give them a chance to live. I plant a leaf without a growth point and wait for months or even a year.

But after months or a year some die. Then I remove it and throw it away because it is dead.

But God does not throw away the dead. God wants to revive the dead and the dying. In His love God gives us life. The Devil tries to kill living people but God raises the dead, and the dying to life.

After three months of heat last summer my backyard grasses have died. I went to buy grass sods to replace the dead grasses. There was none because the demand was high. Then I realized the resurrection in God. I began to pray for my grasses that God may give them resurrection.

God's love is the fountain of all lives.

Life is mysterious. What is life? I have questioned it for a long time and I have not found an answer yet. So I put it as mysterious. A succulent leaf with life is green and grows because it has life in it. A dead leaf turns into a transparent pouch of water because there is no life. Why does life make a transparent pouch of water grow into a green leaf? Why does a green leaf change to a transparent pouch of water without life? I still have no answer.

One thing that I know is that life comes from God.

"The Lord God formed the man from the dust of the ground and breathed into his nostrils the breath of life, and the man became a living being." (Genesis 2:7) When God takes away the breath of life from a living man, the man dies and turns to dust. All living creatures received the gift of life from God. God's love is the fountain of all living creatures.

God gave the commandments of love.

I don't have to mention the selfishness of men. They try to knock down others who are better than themselves. They approach others with malicious intent. They steal other's life savings. They plan a perfect crime and kill others. In order to live in the world I also become hard-hearted.

God is love. God loves such a sinful world and He wants sinful men to learn love. It is hard for evil men to learn love. So God gave commandments of love. When one wants to shoot his enemy, he drops his gun when he remembers God's commandment of love; "Love your enemies." (Matthew 5:44) When one plans to eat delicious foods just for her and her children, she shares the food with hungry neighbors when she remembers God's commandment of love; "Love your neighbor as yourself." (Leviticus 19:18) When two men meet together and they compete with each other; God gives them commandment of love; "Love each other." (John 15:17) The greatest commandment is to love God and to love your neighbor. (Leviticus 19:18, Luke 10:27,28)

As we try to obey these commandments of love with difficulty, even with a forceful way, our eyes open in the world of love. It does not require a lot of money. We can see an opportunity to love. We can speak words of love. We can live as God's children. The love of God spreads through the children of God. Where love is, there is heaven.

Some learn love through loving parents. Orphans have no parents to teach them love. Some learn hatred through their parents. God made all of them to learn love by obeying the commandments of love.

God's love is humble.

What is humility? Humility is lowering one's status for others. Humans are not humble and can not be humble. Why should an excellent human being lower himself to those who live at the lowest bottom? So it is much better to be with people who have similar levels; billionaires with other billionaires, middle class with other middle class, penniless with other penniless.

There are different classes determined by education and intelligence; PhD with other PhDs, Masters with other masters, undereducated with other under educated.

I was in a patient's room. The patient's condition was very serious and the worried family asked the doctor about the patient's condition. The doctor spoke very fast and fluently using professional terminology as if he was speaking to medical students or to other doctors in a seminar. The family was just listening quietly. I did not think that the doctor was proud. It was too hard for him to go down to the level of lay people and explain with the language of lay people.

It was easier for him to speak in his own level of medical knowledge. It was obvious that the doctor and the family were disconnected. It was an undiluted encounter between a highly educated professional and lay people.

But God could talk to the family at the family's level of understanding because God lowers Himself to our level of understanding. He talks to us just like parents lower themselves to a baby's level when they talk to their baby.

I went to a church conference. The main speaker was a Korean seminary professor who spoke English like a native American. He had an amazing career and record in the field of seminary. He did not hide his disgusting feelings toward us who were missionaries from America and Canada. In his eyes we were so ignorant that he could not give any academic lectures. He picked some words we were using and explained why we were using wrong words in ignorance. His four hour main lecture was about his career. He looked down at us. I felt humiliated by his attitude, and that was exactly what he intended to do. It was a conference where I paid money and time just to be humiliated by a seminary professor. Anyway I learned a lesson from him; Don't be proud of yourself. It is ugly.

It seems like he did not study about the humility of God. God is humble. Had God been a speaker that day He might have spoken something to heal our wounds and weaknesses. He would have said something to encourage us to go on. After the conference, we would have left full of faith and spirit.

Humility has the power to move people's hearts. About a year after my arrival to America I was working in a huge surgery department in NYC. There were hundreds of things for me to learn. The surgical team asked me for a supply and I was looking for it in a hurry. One doctor came to me and said; "What are you looking for? I can help you." He was an African American surgeon, and the chief of the residents of the surgery department. As a leader of the residents, he was managing the resistant attitudes of the white residents. I was so moved by his attitude. I found that such a person exists in this world. He lowered himself to a new foreign nurse to help. When I did not bring the requested supplies quickly enough, the surgeons often screamed and hurried to the head nurse to report it.

Jesus lowered Himself from God to human. Among humans, He lowered Himself to the lowest, a servant. Still He lowered Himself again to a falsely accused criminal. Again, He lowered himself to whipping, torture, and ridicule. Finally, He lowered Himself to capital punishment by crucifixion.

Jesus did not look down on sinners. He lowered Himself to any sinner's situation so that we could see Him eye to eye and listen to His humble and loving words without shame or humiliation. Men in high positions, men in low positions, masters, servants, the sad, the hungry, the homeless, the falsely accused, the ridiculed, the whipped, the tortured, the dying with capital punishment............ Jesus was there with them all, Jesus is with them all, and Jesus will be with them.

Humility can not be bought with money. Humility can not be gained by taking classes and examinations. Yet everyone can be humble when he receives the love of Jesus and imitates Jesus. God's love is humble love.

God's love is greater than our sins.

I read this story in Korean TV news. A man and a young boy came to a convenience store. They put milk and some packages of food in their bag and attempted to leave without paying. The owner of the store caught them and called the police.

The police arrived at the scene, and after a brief investigation, it was revealed that the man and the boy were the father and his son. They did not eat for two days. The father lost his job and money ran out before he got another job.

Hearing the story, the owner of the store declined to charge the father and the son. The police took the father and the son outside to a nearby restaurant. And another man was following them behind. The policeman bought them a meal with his own money. They ate the food after starving for two days. While they were still eating, a man entered the restaurant and gave them an envelope with money inside. He was a customer at the convenience store, and saw the whole thing. When the policeman took them outside, he followed them. After he saw the restaurant they entered, he went to a bank, withdrew money, returned to the restaurant, and gave the money to the father and the son. He was a Korean living abroad and he was visiting Korea at that time. Then the people began to bring packages of food to the store to be delivered to the father and the son.

No one wanted to punish them for stealing, but all wanted to help them overcome the time of hardship and build a new life.

This event helped me understand God's love. When we come to God with our sins, does God want to punish us for the sins? No. He removed our sins from us to Jesus and made Jesus be punished. (Isaiah 53:4,5) God helps us overcome the time of hardships and build a new life just as the Korean community did.

I tried to lead a woman to Jesus. Her initial reaction was; "God has so many things to do over the whole world. Don't let God be bothered with me." Years later she said, "I have committed many sins, and I can not go before God." She had a lingering hesitation to go to God. Was she expecting God's anger or punishment? No. God's love is greater than all her sins. God not only forgives her but also wants to rebuild her life with blessings. But she did not surrender herself to the love of God.

Contrarily, I read about a serial killer. He killed over 30 young women. Eventually, he was captured and received a death sentence. He came to God with all his sins. All his sins were removed from him by Jesus. How deep, how high, and how great the love of God is! God's love was greater than all his sins. He preached God's love to other inmates in prison until his execution. I saw his picture of a peaceful face before his execution.

The woman sinned a lot less than the serial killer, she did not kill even one person. But she did not come to God's love. The serial killer sinned a lot more but he came to God. God's love was greater than his sins.

God's love is sacrificial.

"God so loved the world that He gave His one and only Son, that whoever believes in Him shall not perish but have eternal life." John 3:16

It is the climax of love that God sent His one and only Son, Jesus, into this world. This shows the deep world of love humans cannot understand. When we force ourselves to obey God's commandments of love, loving others becomes easier and easier. But there is a limit. We can not lose too much to love others. We can not give too much. We love others within a boundary of safety and affordability. Furthermore, I can not sacrifice my life for others.

God's love is sacrificial love. Jesus sacrificed His life on the cross to save sinners. This love requires a lot of meditation. Think about Jesus who put His life to death and endured the pain of death for almost six hours on the cross. I can not endure such pain for even one second. I ask Jesus; Lord, why did you give your life to death? How did you endure the pain of pierced nails? Jesus did not say anything but I know the answer; It is for you.

God has given us such sacrificial love but did not demand us. God just asked us to believe. We believe and are thankful for Jesus' sacrificial love for us. We believe that Jesus died on the cross with our sins, washed all our sins with His blood, was buried, and was raised from the dead on the third day. He will come back to take us to heaven.

Believing in Jesus or not may be a personal freedom. He who believes has received forgiveness of sins and eternal life, and he who does not believe will serve a life term sentence in a prison of eternal fire. (Mark 9:47,48) In order to save us from the life term sentence in a prison of eternal fire Jesus laid His life to the pain of death. God's love is sacrificial.

Chapter 18:
Forgiveness And Unforgiveness

Each country has its own laws. In Korea, cars have the right of way, and in America, pedestrians have the right of way. In Korea, I followed the Korean traffic laws. And in America, I keep the American traffic laws.

In North Korea, carrying a Bible is a crime of capital punishment. In America, carrying a Bible is not a crime at all. Recently, one American woman was arrested and put in jail in one of the Arab nations because she shouted in the street. Women can not raise their voices loudly in a public place in that nation. It is against the law in that nation.

I have found a huge difference in the interpretation of unforgiveness in this world, and in heaven. In life, we encounter someone who hurt us, ruined our lives, left in our hearts emotional wounds and scars. It is natural to hate such people. We do to our enemies whatever we decide to do; to kill, never forgive, cut relationships, retaliate, and get even, just ignore…………..As a result unforgiveness and hatred remain in the victim's heart.

Jesus explains this situation using a parable of an unmerciful servant in Matthew 18:21-35.

First, let's read 18:28-31. A servant went out and found a fellow servant who owed him 100 denarii. One denari was a day's wage and 100 denarii was 100 days wages. So it was about three months' wages. The creditor servant demanded payment but the debtor servant did not have money. The debtor servant knelt down and begged to give him time. But the creditor servant grabbed the debtor servant and put him in a prison. This is a very normal legal process of a creditor. The creditor wants to recover damages done by the debtor.

When this event is connected with the previous event, it gives a totally different perspective of the creditor. Let's read Matthew 18:23-27. The creditor servant is now a debtor. The king is the creditor. The servant owed the king 10,000 talents. One talent is one year's wage. The servant has to work 10,000 years to pay his debt. So he knelt down on his knees before the king. The king had pity on him and canceled all the debt of 10,000 talents. The king could have recovered some damages by selling the servant, his wife, and his children as slaves. But instead of the usual, normal, and legal process, the king showed mercy and forgiveness to the debtor servant.

The servant was forgiven 10,000 years x 365 denarii = 3,650,000 denarii. What should he do to his fellow servant who owed him 100 denarii? Since he received great mercy for the cancellation of 3,650,000 denarii, he has the moral and ethical responsibility to show some mercy to others. It is like a man who received a cancellation of $3,65 million debt grabs a poor brother's neck who can not pay him $100. Others who watched his actions were greatly distressed and reported it to the king. (Matthew 18:31)

The king called the servant in and said; 'You wicked servant, I canceled all that debt of yours because you begged me to. Shouldn't you have had mercy on your fellow servant just as I had on you?' The servant failed to practice a little mercy and forgiveness after he received a great mercy and forgiveness. The king called it wicked. This is the law in heaven. The angry king revoked the canceled debt. The servant was not worthy of receiving mercy and forgiveness. The king demanded the servant to pay 10,000 talents.

"This is how my heavenly Father will treat each of you unless you forgive your brother from your heart." Matthew 18:35

What does it mean? God will cancel His forgiveness and the unforgiving will lose his own salvation.

After 17 years in America I visited my home town and met my high school friend. She was then a pastor's wife. She asked me; "What would you call the Bible in one word?" I answered, 'love.'

She said, 'forgiveness.' She added that The Bible is the record of how men sinned and how God forgave them their sins.

Then she told me about forgiveness. Her husband was an assistant pastor of a church. But the senior pastor was jealous of her husband and expelled him abruptly. Her family was cut off from all provisions and moved into a storage place. Her family skipped many meals, and whenever they ran out of food, they had fasting prayers.

From the storage space they started a new church. The new church started to grow after they forgave the senior pastor from their hearts. When I met her, their ministry was big.

Forgiveness is not easy. Ask Jesus how hard it was to forgive us. Nails crushed his bones in his hands and feet. (Isaiah 53:5) He was tortured. He was misunderstood, ridiculed, and jeered. He went through the pains of death. How hard it was to forgive sinners! Forgiveness is not easy and natural. We also need some difficulties and self denial to forgive and reconcile. And we need to do it so as not to lose our own salvation.

The words of my friend made me think about my own unforgiveness. I had an enemy that I could not forgive. My enemy destroyed my marriage life and drove my family into destitution.

My family visited Houston as the newly assigned mission field, and we drove back to Toledo, Ohio, to our home. At that time, there was a blizzard in the area of Ohio, and over 20 people died in the freezing cold. It was the end of February in 1990. All major expressways were closed. My children and I had no winter coats, and we kept ourselves warm with the heat coming out of the car heater.

To make a long story short, my family miraculously survived the blizzard and arrived home in the evening. My home was empty. The back door to the kitchen was broken. One window was broken, and sub zero cold wind was coming into the house through the broken window, and the heater was working non stop. Some trash was blowing on the living room floor by the wind. All our possessions were gone, and the whole house was empty.

Without our permission, the church people broke the back door and moved all our belongings to a truck. We were told that the truck was broken and couldn't move. Our family went to the place where the truck was parked. I went inside the truck to find any winter coats or blankets, but I could not find any among the furniture and packages.

My family had to sleep somewhere that night. We couldn't ask any of the church members to shelter us that night. I called one American nurse who studied the Bible with me. She welcomed our family and provided us with one room for the night. She gave her daughter's winter coats to my daughters and one of her coats to me. She also gave me some money. I have not talked to her ever since, and I have not paid back her kindness until now. She was a good Samaritan to our family that night.

The next day, we had to drive back to Houston without any belongings. Before we left, we drove around our home three times and said, "Good bye, our home. Good bye forever!" Next one week our family lived in our van and in motels. We moved into a rented home but had nothing with us. The truck with our belongings arrived in Houston at our rented house. It took two weeks from the day they loaded the truck with our belongings to arrive in Houston at our rented home. They excused the delay due to the truck problems. How could initially they bring a broken truck to my house and why was it broken after they loaded it with my belongings?

There were hardships, but my family endured. I didn't shed one drop of tears because I felt that my family would collapse if they saw me crying.

One day I was at work in a hospital. I told my patient about this incident. In the middle of my talking, he stopped me and asked me. "Did you say that this happened in a church?" I answered, "Yes, in a church I used to go." He responded, "It can not be a church." He meant that this could happen in a criminal group, not in a church.

I still remember every single moment when my family and I went through the blizzard without winter coats and blankets. But I could never connect this event with God's mercy and the forgiveness I received from God. To me, it was a separate event. God's forgiveness was one thing and hating my enemy was another. According to Jesus the two events are connected. When these two events are connected, my position is changed from a victim to a wicked servant because of my unforgiveness towards my enemy. I will be found unworthy of receiving God's forgiveness. Furthermore, I will lose my salvation if I persist in my unforgiveness.

I turned my attention to God's mercy 3,650,000 times more than I have to offer my mercy of 100 to my enemy. How can I feel and grasp God's mercy of 3,650,000 denarii for me? How big is God's mercy for me? I calculated this way and that way but I could not have any concept of it.

A few days ago I went outside early in the morning while it was still dark. The temperature was in the low 60's. The air was cool and fresh. I felt this cool air before the hot summer started months ago. I enjoyed it while breathing in and out deeply.

Suddenly an inspiration came into my heart that God's mercy and forgiveness was like the fresh air I was breathing in and out. It is like the air. The air filled over the whole backyard, over the whole Houston city, over the whole earth, over the trees, birds, and animals. God is merciful over all His creatures, over men and women, over all sinners. Every time I breathe, I breathe God's mercy. God's mercy was not in millions of numbers but in the air, like the air. God's mercy spreads and covers all the world like the waters in the ocean. How great the mercy of God is! God forgave us and He wants us to forgive. This is the law of heaven. It is the kingdom of mercy and forgiveness.

In this world, unforgiveness is an emotional matter of victim but in heaven it is a sin of wickedness. The unforgiving servant was legally correct but ethically wicked. Last thirty three years, no one came to me saying, "I am sorry, please, forgive me." But now it doesn't matter. I forgive them all. I will erase the bitterness and I will enjoy God's mercy and forgiveness over all the creatures.

On our way of life we can trip over and have an injury. But with mercy and forgiveness, our wound heals. We can get up and continue our life journey toward eternal life saying; because Jesus forgave me, I forgive you, too.

Made in United States
Troutdale, OR
07/17/2025